# CHINDIT COLUMN

# CHINDIT COLUMN

Charles Carfrae

WILLIAM KIMBER · LONDON

First published in 1985 by
WILLIAM KIMBER & CO. LIMITED
100 Jermyn Street, London, SW1Y 6EE

® Charles Carfrae, 1985
ISBN 0-7183-0555-8

Typeset by Jubal Multiwrite
and printed in Great Britain by
The Garden City Press Limited
Letchworth, Hertfordshire, SG6 1JS

# Contents

# List of Illustrations

# List of Maps

To my comrades-in-arms, black and
white, in Nigeria and Burma, 1940–1944

# Author's Note

Many pages of military autobiography, often in self-justification, have been written by generals of greater or lesser eminence; fewer by junior and obscure professional officers without an axe to grind. I hope that this book may prove of some interest as a description of one young man's life during the Second World War within the framework of an empire soon to be dismantled. Most of the material was first drafted many years ago, when incident and detail remained fresh in mind; and for every one then recorded on paper, the process of rewriting has restored to memory half a dozen others. Nothing has been included that is not true; in so far, that is, as truth may be discerned through subjective eyes.

In an attempt to reproduce the texture of the Northern Nigerian's Hausa speech I have translated it as literally as makes sense. Much of the character and spirit of such dialogue would, I feel, be lost if it were to be put into everyday idiomatic English.

A few names have been changed but only one (clearly indicated) from Chapter Six on.

# CHAPTER 1
## An Uncertain Young Officer

In 1934, at the age of eighteen, I found myself, somewhat to my surprise, at Sandhurst. Though grandfather, father, uncle and elder brother were, or had been, career soldiers, at preparatory and public schools I had felt no notable enthusiasm for military life. Nor did I display aptitude for any other. A family disappointment, I drifted dreamily through childhood and adolescence, such school friends as I possessed mostly of the sort who liked to label themselves, grandly, as intellectuals. For myself I remained a nonentity, poor and timid at games, too stupid or too indolent to pass examinations and in the end forced to leave early in order to be crammed for Sandhurst. A marked tendency to look on rather than participate is of little advantage to a youth destined by profession to become a man of action.

Sandhurst, said to have been described by the headmaster of a neighbouring public school as 'that hell over the hill', was indeed initially alarming; but though Royal Military College discipline would have struck any objective observer as fierce and rigid to a degree, only the most aesthetic could have claimed Sandhurst to be a hell. The 'gentlemen cadets', as we were politely called, appeared undamaged by a regimen that few modern youths from any walk of life would put up with for a moment unless it were for money.

One cannot truthfully suggest that pre-war Sandhurst did much, in a direct way, to train its cadets to become good officers, or indeed officers of any category. But if it be true that to lead others a young man must first learn to obey, all concerned saw to it that he did so instantly. We found ourselves condemned to hours of toil polishing to an unnatural perfection rifle butts, bayonet scabbards, leather belts and boots in what was said to be our spare time; spending set periods in activities such as horsemanship, gymnasium exercises and – above all – drill; being forced to make lightning changes from one 'order of dress' to another so as not to appear late on parade. Several times a week our officers (remote beings) instructed us, at a less breathless pace, in strategy and tactics and also in military history, all from the viewpoint of an army or corps commander, a status so exalted that only one in many hundreds of cadets would

achieve it, and he thirty years or more after being commissioned.
Where we excelled was in glisteningly irreproachable turn-out and
close-order drill. No Guards regiment could hold a candle to us. The
precision, the panache, the simultaneous crunch of boots, the resounding, perfectly synchronised crash of palms on rifle slings: these were
splendid to see and hear. Our drill masters, selected warrant
officers and senior NCOs from the Foot Guards, men who could
have made a troop of baboons jump to it, had voices that carried for
miles and could call on time-hallowed idioms and phrases from the
Caterham parade ground appropriate for every contingency.

'Number three company – Shun! Asyerwere! Shun! Asyerwere!
Shun! Asyerwere! Is your foot stuck, Mr Dalgleish, sir? Move, sir.
*Move*! You're idle, Mr Dalgleish.'

'Hit those rifles, 'it 'em! Don't stroke 'em like they were
pussy cats!'

'Mr Viscount Buckfastleigh, don't sway, sir. There's no wind, sir,
and you're not in the chorus, not yet. You, Mr Webber sir, keep
your face to attention! Wipe it off! Nothing I say is funny, sir.'

When not required for drill or other instruction we would
exchange uniforms for the tweed jackets, dark grey flannel trousers,
trilbys or flat tweed caps that were de rigueur, using bicycles (known
as 'bogwheels') for transport to and from the pubs and cinemas of
Camberley and Blackwater. Whether in plain clothes or uniform,
on bogwheels or briskly walking, all gentlemen cadets looked remarkably similar one to another – clean, short-haired, fresh-faced and fit,
bodies perhaps in better trim than minds, which fortunately for
some of us were less extended.

Sandhurst life was not all disciplined severity. Regular dances
enhanced existence for the bolder spirits and there would be the
annual June Ball, ourselves neat in blue patrol uniform with little
brass buttons and our officers glorious in scarlet mess kit. Every
cadet who fancied himself anything of a ladies' man would invite
the most beautiful creature he knew, or even one he scarcely knew
at all, for the sake of personal prestige. Always it would be
rumoured that some famous actress or other was to honour us with
her presence, but of course she never did.

The great majority of us were products of the better-known public
schools. Candidates assessed as 'not quite the right type' – a favourite
phrase – by the Interviewing Board were, so it was alleged, cunningly given the minimum pass mark for that important part of the
entrance examination rather than being turned down flat. A very low

interview score ensured that a candidate striking the board as unlikely to maintain the dignity of arms could never, unless a genius, scrape up enough marks on the written papers to secure entrance. Nobody could openly accuse the examiners of snobbery: the young man, having passed the interview, had failed overall and that was that!

It is difficult to write seriously of Sandhurst; we put up with it, more or less cheerfully, as an interlude between school and real life. In no respect did I shine, failing to achieve the rank of cadet under-officer, sergeant or even corporal, though so far as one's future career was concerned this didn't matter in the least. I got drunk several times, kissed and fondled a handful of girls (at least one of them a younger edition of Betjeman's Joan Hunter-Dunn), drove at high speed to London and back in a beautiful green Bentley which I didn't own, read poetry and picked up live adders by the tail on Barossa Common, a trick learnt years before.

After the eighteen month Sandhurst course I duly 'passed out' and early in 1936, shortly before my twentieth birthday, was commissioned into a Light Infantry regiment, joining its 2nd Battalion at Colchester. On the same day two other new second lieutenants arrived, one from Cambridge University, the other from the supplementary reserve, or 'back door', both of whom seemed to settle down well enough. I failed dismally to settle down at all and the following eight months stand out as the blackest of my life. The tide had carried me where it would and I had drifted with it, managing to close my eyes to the future even as late as Sandhurst. Curiously, it was some comment of the London tailor's where I was being fitted for my various uniforms that suddenly faced me with the fact that all boats had been burnt. I had, willy nilly, become a commissioned officer in His Majesty's Land Forces.

My company commander, Williams, a subaltern nearing middle-age, filled me with dread. What he thought of me he expressed repeatedly in unambiguous terms: I was an ignorant, wet and utterly useless second lieutenant, the worst he had yet seen, unfitted to be an officer in his regiment or indeed any other. Though I found myself in no position to quarrel with this assessment I would have welcomed some small crumbs of explanation, advice or encouragement.

'Carfrae, what are you doing? Damn-all, I suppose, except scratching your arse as usual. Be at the butts on C range at 10.30. Tell Sergeant White to find a butt party. Do you know what to take with you?'

'No, sir, not exactly.'

'Then bloody well find out. You're to mark targets for some competition the Fusiliers are having. Do you know how to organise things at the butts?'

'I've never done it. No.'

'Haven't you learnt anything at all? Well, find that out, too. Sergeant White knows all right. There's something else – when you go to an all ranks' dance your job is to dance with the company NCOs' wives, not with town tarts and treat them to port and lemon after. We don't do that in the Regiment.'

'I'm sorry. I only danced with one girl. She was on her own.'

'You're a bloody liar as well as useless. You were dancing with them all last night. I'm not blind!'

Writing thus of Williams, who loomed over my life like the shadow of Frankenstein's monster, makes me feel a prick of guilt. No doubt I asked for a great deal of what I received; no doubt Williams' was the attitude he thought correct, his treatment the best way to make something out of an unpromising officer, his hostility a mask assumed for my own good. Williams himself, perhaps, had been dealt with in similar fashion after joining the regiment fifteen or sixteen years earlier. Certainly the adjutant's opinion of me stood no higher. This dignitary, a magnificently smart, coldly handsome subaltern with an upturned reddish moustache, the archetypal image of a British officer and a man of whom the junior subalterns felt considerably in awe, I found it safer to admire from a distance. In all respects falling short of Hilman's standards, I trembled with apprehension whenever he addressed me.

That autumn I heard that I was due for posting to our 1st Battalion in India, which news contributed little towards raising my spirits. Though I would escape from Williams, it seemed possible that frying pan was to be exchanged for fire.

The 1st Battalion's Indian station was Poona, about seventy miles up-country from Bombay. The very name 'Poona', to those of my generation, was held to epitomise the Raj at its most absurd; the grotesque world of pukka sahibs and memsahibs, chota pegs, salaams, polo, Wolseley sun helmets and dusky Gunga Dins it suggested could always be depended on to raise smiles. People in England refused to believe that such a place actually existed, and young officers attending courses there made a point of writing let-

ters home on 'Poona Club' headed paper to convince friends and
relations that it did.

At Poona railway station I was instructed to form up the draft of
men that three brother officers and I had taken out with us and,
steered by a guide sent from the battalion, to march the young
soldiers to cantonments as strange to them as to me. Dusk was falling, turning quickly to dark; the air felt soft, warm but lifeless. The
smells, the pungent, exciting, often disgusting smells of India, at
once enthralled: the smells of ghee and leaf-tobacco smoke, of cor-
iander and burning cowdung, of charcoal and excrement, sandalwood and spices. From trees and bushes by the roadside a
thousand crickets shrilled, their mechanical music a perennial
ingredient of tropical night. But though these first evening impres-
sions remain as vivid as the memory of early love-making, very
soon the smells, the singing of insects at night, became so familiar a
feature of Indian life that they would never be noticed unless stinks
should for some reason be absent or the tireless crickets cease
from chirping.

My platoon of thirty men, some of whom were old sweats, had, of
course, to be instructed what next to do, but seldom how to do it.
They knew better than myself, the men regarding their greenhorn
officer, I suspected, with amused tolerance, though discipline
ensured that little hint of it would be shown. Only on Christmas
Day was there relaxation. There had to be; traditionally, as a matter
of annual routine, half the soldiers would be drunk. 'You ain't too
bad a bloke, Charlie boy!' one of my platoon informed me at
Christmas 1936. He swayed on his feet, blue, unfocussed eyes staring
solemnly into mine; I walked away frowning disapproval but secretly quite pleased. Far from being a competent map reader, I constantly mislaid myself and my men when we were out on our own
and remember an occasion when, training over for the day, I happened for a change to be heading in the right direction for camp.
The soldiers, very softly, started up a song and recognising a
familiar tune I took no notice until my ear caught unfamiliar words.
'Charlie 'asn't lost us, Charlie 'asn't lost us . . .' No 5 Platoon was
singing. I strode on, pretending not to hear.

The British soldier in India between the wars lived much as in
Kipling's day, though his 'Soldiers Three' had more than their fair
share of fighting Pathans on the Frontier. During my two and a half
years in India ours saw neither active service nor 'internal security'
duties, interesting distractions consequently being limited. The

men spent their ample leisure hours dozing on their beds, waving away flies and continually calling for tea from the 'charwallah'; drinking beer at the canteen until the week's pay had gone; swimming, playing football, basketball or cricket; walking out with Anglo-Indian girls ('chi-chis') or stealthily visiting Indian prostitutes in the town, who as likely as not would present them with doses of VD. Pay for the week, derisory, would be soon spent. Once a fortnight organised games of 'House' (much the same as Bingo) drew crowds of soldiers, sessions having to be supervised by the Entertainments Officer, myself for a spell. The caller, the sergeant-major of my own company, a burly warrant-officer with hooded eyes and a frog-like expression, pocketed at intervals a handful of jingling rupees so openly that in my innocence I thought it part of the game. It was not.

As well as ourselves there were stationed in the Poona cantonments a second British infantry battalion (which of course we considered militarily and socially inferior to our own), two Punjabi battalions and one of Indian Cavalry. The Indian Cavalry, mostly still horse remained a picturesque corps, its officers – they wore marvellously elaborate mess dress embellished with frogging and gold or silver lace – considering themselves elevated above the common run. Dashing and careless, given to polo and pig-sticking, they faithfully echoed the faintly supercilious, drawling, insouciant air cultivated by their British equivalents. The very names of Indian cavalry regiments resounded with 'John Company' history and Ouida romance: Skinner's Horse, Sam Browne's Cavalry, The Bengal Lancers, Hodson's Horse, The Guides Cavalry.

I made several friends outside the regimental circle, one of them a young Indian army officer called Bobby Pringle, arresting in appearance with tow-coloured hair, bright blue eyes and a Grecian nose. An Oxford graduate, dreamer rather than man of action, a lover of poetry and the romantic, Bobby was second-in-command of a Pathan company, his swash-buckling, hatchet-faced and bloodthirsty soldiers fascinating him. Francis Stuart – also in a Punjabi regiment – whom I had known in England, visited Poona for a Signals course. Francis, shy and quiet, lacked Bobby's open ebullience but had considerable sensitivity and depth of feeling. He kept and trained peregrine and saker falcons (those fierce, fathomless black eyes!) and took me out hawking for partridges and doves on the scorched plains near the Towers of Silence, on the tops of which Parsees exposed their dead and where flocks of vultures ceaselessly soared and wheeled, dark against the sun, hoping for fresh corpses to augment piles of bleaching human bones.

I was next to meet Francis in the Burma forests in 1944. Bobby, a shooting star, vanished I know not where.

Slow to adapt myself to military life, for the first year or so in India I could scarcely be considered more of a regimental asset than I had been at Colchester. None of my seniors, however, went out of their way to rub it in; they treated me kindly, indeed generously, though by common consent I proved unfortunate in both my first two company commanders. It began to look as though like peoples and their bosses I got the superiors I deserved.

After two and a half years, I feel ashamed to confess to having known less of the real India than an alert visitor might have discovered for himself in as many months, and have frequently reproached myself since for making so little of opportunities and living so myopic a life. In extenuation it can be said that four out of five officers in the British service proved equally unenterprising. I had shot fur and feather, including a tiger; I was familiar with many birds, reptiles, butterflies and moths; but of Indians themselves I learnt little indeed. Apart from a beautiful and English-educated girl called Miss Jinnah I had spoken to no Indian lady that I can remember. Newly-commissioned Indian officers, Hindu and Moslem, would be attached to the regiment from time to time before joining the Indian Army and lived on equal terms with us, but so fearful were they of committing social blunders, so intent on assimilating British customs and military etiquette that they revealed little of themselves.

At about the time of my twenty-third birthday in March 1939 I was granted eight months' home furlough, leaving in Poona practically everything I possessed. War was to intervene; chattels and trophies disappeared for ever. Having held the King's Commission for three years now, I remained deficient in confidence, introspective but not friendless, fitting in tolerably well but not yet perfectly adapted. If vague thoughts of a different career persisted less, there were times when I regretted not being quite the stamp of young man thought well of by public school housemasters, muscular Christians, red-tabbed senior officers, masters of hounds and other personages of that ilk. Dashing horsemen or athletes possessing a cheerful and modestly self confident manner went down best in the old peacetime army. 'Fine young chap, you're lucky to have him,' brigadier might say to colonel of such a paragon, almost at first glance. I don't think it was said of me. Nonetheless by now I had learnt something of my profession and felt perfectly satisfied with the colonel's final comment on my latest confidential report, which read: 'With more experience should make a very useful officer,' or something to that effect.

The buoyant months of leave in England blew away one by one, like coloured soap bubbles released by a child; but only the most blinkered could have failed to perceive the gathering clouds and many weeks before my leave was due to end I read without surprise the War Office telegram instructing me to report immediately at the Regimental Depot. I chanced to be sitting in the mess there when Chamberlain made the speech telling Britain she was at war.

After three weeks of doing various odd jobs – not the only young officer of the regiment caught up by the war whilst on leave – I was dispatched by the War Office to Farnborough as adjutant of a newly forming Officer Cadet Training Unit, with the rank of temporary captain. A month earlier the idea of being made either a captain or an adjutant at twenty-three would have been laughable; but promotion of a temporary nature is thrust upon most professional officers in wartime. It came quickly simply because I happened to be a spare man.

In Poona I had done virtually no paper work; at Farnborough I was to be engaged in little else. Accustomed while at duty to dealing only with NCOs and men, most of my contacts were now with officers. Instead of being always at the receiving end of admonition, I myself admonished even company commanders, acting of course on behalf of my colonel. Of the OCTU staff, gathered together from Guards and line regiments and an uneasy mix of regular, reservist and territorial, at least one officer had worn no uniform since 1918, while the most junior had little more military knowledge than the cadets they were supposed to instruct. But since the OCTU bore little or no resemblance to Sandhurst we could at least hope that the emergency-commissioned officers turned out would know better how to lead platoons in action. Life a perpetual rush, nothing was ever carried out quite as thoroughly as it should have been; always one had to be getting on with something else equally important.

With deplorable celerity I turned myself into the most pernickety and absurd of bureaucrats, having a special rubber stamp made with my signature in facsimile upon it, buying elegant 'in', 'out' and 'pending' boxes painted in light infantry green and insisting that any letter or paper prepared for signature on which even a smear showed must be re-typed. Only Salisbury, my orderly room sergeant, a patient, charming and supremely efficient man from the Queen's regiment, prevented me from destroying myself with long hours and worry, much of it over trifles. To work in the orderly room clerks' office as an 'authorised civilian typist' – she happened to be a very good one – I carefully introduced my current love, whose home lay near, and made a point of visiting the clerks' room daily on some pretext or other to watch her slender neck leaning over the typewriter, admire her dark hair and dark eyes with their long lashes, her tender upper lip and young boy's profile. But within weeks Kate had allied herself with the soldier clerks instead of her admirer. I became merely the boss, almost an enemy, to be quickly deserted for another officer, a young peacetime barrister with a plausible manner. Knowing nothing of this affair in its early stages, by chance one morning I noticed a letter for him in the officers' mess rack, its envelope addressed in the familiar hand that had quickened my heart-beats for many a month. It was a very bitter moment.

After completing my year's stint as adjutant of the OCTU, without the least reluctance I handed over to a successor in August and returned to the Regimental Depot as a subaltern again. With little to do, and certainly nothing of importance, I became so bored and restless that a contemporary, David Darnley, and I made a solemn agreement that we would volunteer for the next job on offer provided it was certain to take us abroad. Volunteers for every kind of duty used frequently to be called for in the early years of war and within a month we found ourselves in London, captive of one of those dreadful toadstool growths spawned by hostilities, a transit hotel we were not supposed to leave.

David and I had volunteered, and been accepted, for service with the Royal West African Frontier Force.

# CHAPTER 2

# Nigerian Rifle Company

A shabby cargo vessel of the Elder-Dempster line carried us two, with a dozen other officers, to West Africa in the second October of the war. Now that the moment for leaving Liverpool had actually arrived my heart felt unaccountably heavy. I didn't regret having volunteered and had left nobody behind from whom I couldn't bear to part; but England, even wartime England, seemed suddenly precious. Leaning over the ship's rails I gazed at the drab warehouses and deserted quayside without seeing them, hardly conscious of the water's neutral slap against the ship's hull and the cries of drifting gulls.

We began our voyage in convoy, torrents of bitterly cold rain screening the other ships in it from view, but in the course of a day or two the weather cleared and one night the vessel nearest, the *City of Benares*, was torpedoed. She had been transporting children towards supposed safety in America. Horrified, we watched the ship drifting astern, growing smaller and smaller, all her lights blazing as though it were peacetime still and she on a holiday cruise. Our senior officer, a swarthy major, had urged the captain to stop – to pick up any surviving children at whatever risk; but he had refused point blank. His orders were clear, he said: his vessel must keep going, come what might. It was the closest most of us had been to war.

When the ship eventually steamed into Freetown Harbour, Sierra Leone, we all crowded the deck to gaze at this new country. The air felt very hot and humid; haze blurred the outlines of pale, peeling houses but we could make out black-faced figures, gnomes at that distance, walking or cycling along the sea road. The forests on the dominating hills flaunted a green almost viridian; the whole scene, unfolding as we drew closer, one of colour and vivacity, quite different from the muted tones of India, the lethargy and sense of timelessness. Freetown was a garishly-tinted picture postcard.

When a motor launch took us to shore to stretch our legs we passed close to the bloated body of a white sailor, drifting face down and dark with flies. The many small craft in the harbour must either have failed to observe or deliberately ignored the corpse. It was a shocking introduction, putting picture postcards out of mind.

In the streets we were assailed by a powerful stink in which no trace of Eastern sandalwood or spice could be detected. There was much bustle and movement, Africans laughing and smiling constantly and shouting at one another, the women, inclined to stoutness, wearing brightly printed cottons while the men, less gaudy, favoured white or khaki shorts below flying shirt tails. Swarms of pot-bellied little boys and girls, winking and leering in the most suggestive way imaginable, followed us everywhere until David and I felt driven to seek refuge in a hotel bar. There we saw some officers of the Royal West African Frontier Force we were about to join. Evidently having no pressing duty to perform they were drinking beer, very smart in well-starched khaki drill with black palm tree badges on the open collars of their shirts. On a table we noticed wide bush hats decorated with bunches of feather hackle. David and I, our own ship-creased drill innocent of brave insignia, stood about self-consciously until whisked away from the hotel and taken to the Sierra Leone Regiment's officers' mess by, of all people, Hilman – a major now – the awe-inspiring 2nd Battalion adjutant of Colchester days. He entertained us most courteously and if, as I fancied, Hilman looked down his nose as disapprovingly as ever I may have been mistaken.

In Freetown harbour the battleship *Barham*, damaged by the French during the recent Dakar fiasco, lay at anchor, the first capital ship I had set eyes on. Had the drowned sailor, I wondered, been one of her crew? Huge and grey, motionless, painted ship on painted ocean, she filled the view from Hilman's mess veranda.

Off Accra I lost David and wished him good fortune, he posted to the Gold Coast Regiment and I to the Nigeria. Obviously nothing but a chance pencil stroke against a name on a list determined one's West African destination. The ship sailed on until it reached the mangrove forests concealing Lagos. No other man disembarked there; I stood forlornly on the wharf watching the palm trees swaying on the shore line until discovered by a staff officer who, consulting a piece of paper, instructed me to board the train for Kaduna, five hundred miles to the north. I took a taxi to the Lagos railway siding. Darkness had fallen, fireflies wove everchanging patterns round the tree-tops and choirs of bass-voiced frogs grunted from marsh and mangrove swamp with as treble accompaniment the familiar, passionless song of crickets. I felt lonely and friendless as a small boy departing for the first time in school.

The morning after my arrival at Kaduna I skirted the big parade ground on my way to D Company of the 5th Battalion, Nigeria Regiment. Squatting in the dust were a number of young black men being instructed in the English tongue by an African NCO who evidently understood little more of it than they. In chorus and with appropriate gesture, loudly but not at all convincingly, the men chanted after him 'thees my feet', 'thees my hand', 'thees my arse', 'thees my eye', 'thees my belly' and so on. It couldn't but impress a newcomer as a very curious spectacle and I began to wonder what on earth I had let myself in for. Nothing remotely like the scene before me had formed part of my military experience to date: these chanting youths surely not soldiers but slaves in the Zanzibar market of a hundred years before, Nubians from *Arabian Nights* or symbolic figures from some incomprehensible surrealist drama. All were naked to the waist, bare heads closely shaved and dark skins shining with sweat.

Walking into D Company office I saluted my company commander, a Captain Jones. For years a colonial service district officer in the Northern bush, a fluent Hausa speaker who must have known all about his men, Jones felt out of his element as a soldier, a state of affairs he made not the least attempt to disguise. Rising from behind a desk awash with bits of paper, he grasped my hand with the desperation of a drowning man clutching at a straw.

His African clerk, inquisitive, eyed me from a table.

'Ah, Carfrae – a regular subaltern at last!' he said. 'I don't mind telling you, between ourselves, that I know damn-all about this kind of caper. I mean army ways of doing things, and office bumph.'

Flinging wide his arms, he indicated his desk. Several papers fluttered to the floor. 'Yes,' he continued, 'I'm keen enough, but – '

A young officer came in and asked Jones what the company was supposed to be doing next. My company commander frowned.

'Let me think. Oh yes, give them some drill – good thing.'

'They've just finished drill, sir.'

'Have they? Well then, Carfrae, what shall I give them to do?'

Knowing absolutely nothing of his men or their state of training, I had no more idea than he. But I had to say something; the reputation of the regular army lay in my hands.

'Fire control orders, sir,' I replied.

'What are they? Yes, of course. Fire control orders. Hear that, Anderson?'

'Yes sir.'

Anderson, a bespectacled subaltern, saluted and went out, obviously puzzled. A moment before I had seen him personally issuing recruits with uniforms from the quartermaster sergeant's stores.

'Well, that's settled. Now look, Carfrae, what should I do about this?'

Jones displayed a pithy letter from the adjutant making it plain that D Company commander's administrative capability was not highly regarded, and I helped the harassed man to compose an answer. If it had done nothing else, my year as OCTU adjutant had taught me how to deal with a variety of military correspondence and my company commander felt delighted with the apologia we at length fudged between us.

'I'll just keep away for a few days while you put everything straight,' said Jones, within the hour returning to his wife and bungalow. I seldom saw him during the short spell I remained nominally under his command.

The Royal West African Frontier Force, responsible for the maintenance of 'internal security', had before the war been entrusted with a ceremonial role also, like that of the Brigade of Guards, its long-service black soldiers of imposing height and physique, extremely smart, well-disciplined and well-drilled but not encouraged to develop initiative. Immediately pre-war, three or four regular battalions, trained and led by white volunteers from British regiments, had garrisoned Nigeria under the auspices of the Colonial Office. Pay and allowance had been good and cheap polo an attraction for the horsey. During the First World War Nigerians had fought against Germans and their black colonial troops both in East Africa and the Cameroons, a few old Cameroon soldiers still on the active list even in my day having served under the enemy. (One ancient fellow could never understand why he should be forbidden to wear German campaign medals. He had earned them, hadn't he?) The regular Nigerian Brigade having again been despatched to the other side of Africa, this time to fight half-hearted Italians or their auxiliaries in Somaliland and Ethiopia, to fill the vacuum new battalions were rapidly being assembled to counter possible trouble from the Vichy-loyal French possessions by which the Nigerian Protectorate felt itself ominously ringed. Should French troops remain passive, these Nigerian battalions, when ready, might prove useful in some future imperial campaign. A cadre of experienced

Nigerian NCOs had been extracted from the regular units to provide backbone and professional instruction for the expanding
Nigerian formations.

Since the central Regimental Depot for recruits no longer existed, the war-emergency battalions had to find and train their men
as best they might. None was conscripted. Dazzled by the authority
and ceremonial scarlet of recruiting parties despatched to town and
village, young men would place their thumb prints on attestation
papers without, perhaps, quite understanding the significance of
their action; but once enlisted and given uniforms, full bellies and
money, they offered in return unquestioning and loyal service.
Soldiers would be obtained not only by recruiting parties – which
couldn't possibly range over the whole of Northern Nigeria – but by
local chieftains at the instigation of British district officers. It might
be suggested, for example, that fifty tribesmen from X District
would be welcomed by the army, in the time-honoured way all concerned in the business making sure that those who enlisted should
be men whose absence wouldn't much matter. By some such
means must English feudal levies have been raised in medieval
days. Northern Nigeria indeed remained feudal both in spirit and
plain fact; the British, following Lord Lugard's policy, ruled not
directly but through the great Fulani Emirs, maintaining the system
of government found in being when they 'pacified' the country.

Two battalions of the Nigeria Regiment were stationed at Kaduna,
the 5th and the 10th, the latter, though nearly complete, still in the
process of forming. The Kaduna polo ground, immense, was
shared by both and provided every company with more space than
it could possibly need for drill, weapon training and other facets of
the military art not involving a couple of minutes' march to the
adjacent bush.

Surrounding the settlement like a green ocean, and thinly pop-
ulated by pagan Gwarais living in hut-clusters near patches of rude
cultivation, the orchard bush was all-pervasive, low hills, crowned
with black rocks sparsely tenanted by baboons, relieving the
horizon line from flat miles of small, gnarled and evenly spaced
trees. A red laterite road twisted northward seventy miles to Zaria,
an ancient city ruled by an Emir; Hausa traders, local pagans and
slender, nomadic Fulani driving herds of long-horned cattle having
tramped it more or less smooth. All such travellers carried archaic-
looking bows and arrows as token defence against highway

robbery. In the bush piebald hornbills flew from tree to tree in a series of loops, wings creaking like rusty hinges, immense bills giving them a ludicrous, top-heavy aspect; coral-coloured and blue bee-eaters pursued insects and the citadels of termites, pinnacles, pyramids and high spires of cemented earth, stood red between the trees, eroded ruins of Lilliputian architecture. At midday the bush, very hot and very silent, lay crushed under the sun's weight.

I spent much of my brief period with D Company moving from squad to squad to discover what sort of training the African privates were getting and the level of competence one might expect from their instructors, seeing little out of the common apart from those extraordinary English lessons (later to be quietly dropped). It soon became evident, however, that the Nigerian NCO preferred talk to physical demonstration, the sergeants' loud explanatory voices, reinforced by gestures italianate in style, rising and falling interminably while their men gazed at them half-mesmerised, like a church congregation at their preacher during a routine sermon. Many of the regular NCOs had a smattering of English picked up during their service, but few spoke it with fluency and fewer still could read any language. When afternoon duties were over the African sergeant-major would parade his black understrappers outside the company office and instructions for the following day's work be announced by the British sergeant-major in Hausa, or as near as he could get to it. Nothing, no smallest detail, would be forgotten by the Nigerian NCOs, the vastly superior memory of the illiterate convincingly demonstrated time after time.

I remained no more than a fortnight with the 5th Battalion before being transferred across the parade ground to the 10th as a company commander, rank of temporary captain restored. The idea of looking after a fair-sized body of men, whether white, brown or black, appealed infinitely more than the closely supervised paper routine of some junior staff appointment. I was now twenty-four and had developed some degree of confidence, though still inclined to envy (whilst mocking) the hearty and cocksure, drinking and extravert type of regular officer. Men secretly uncertain tend to grow a protective carapace and mine had begun to harden, a process hastened by widening experience and the peculiar, insensitive atmosphere engendered by war.

My B Company, not far short of its complement of over a hundred black soldiers, most of whom were young half-trained recruits, was organised and armed much like any other, Imperial or

British, but possessed both a British and an African sergeant-major, a British but no native colour sergeant and, in theory, British as well as Nigerian platoon sergeants. White platoon sergeants, not only superfluous but on the whole of poor quality, happened mercifully to be in short supply and often I had none on the books. The company clerk, an African civilian from the Gold Coast called Annang or, as he preferred it, Mr Annang, was moderately efficient; he used to write me high-flown 'literary' letters I wish I had kept. He fancied himself many degrees superior to the rank and file, the soldiers for their part thinking nearly as highly of Mr Annang as he did of himself, which however irritating went some way towards proving the truth of the adage that others will take you at your own valuation. I remember a practice air-raid alarm in the course of which this gentleman was forced to take cover in a trench with the rest of the company. 'What, sir? Am I to lie in the self-same trench with these dirty dogs?' he protested.

At first, embarrassingly, I failed to distinguish one black man from another, but after a few weeks wondered how I could ever have made errors. African features, naturally enough, vary as much as European; what is more, every black man's face has its white counterpart. Sule Katsina resembled my friend Bill Knott; Abu Gwandu looked, or looked to me, the image of Corporal White of my old carrier platoon in India. To an extent greater than many people are prepared to admit features reflect character, and certainly one could deduce much from a Nigerian soldier's.

The word 'negro' conjures up a mental picture of a blackish-skinned, well-proportioned man with tightly curled hair, broad nose and big mouth with everted lips. Nigerians from certain southern tribes did indeed approach the stereotype; but hardly a man from B or any other company of the battalion belonged to these. Military policy was to recruit none but 'Northerners'. Popular disturbance was thought more likely to occur in the south and therefore best quelled by Hausa-speaking Northerners; southern tribes, after centuries of contact with European trading men, from slavers on, being considered 'too clever by half' and potential mischiefmakers. Lacking martial virtues, however they might be defined, Southerners would be found to fail as fighting men. Thus theory; its validity, so far as I know, never tested. Certainly true, however, was that 'Northerner' and 'Southerner' represented cultures mutually antipathetic. Only as signaller, vehicle driver or the like would Yoruba or Ibo be enlisted; since he spoke pidgin English it was illogically supposed he must have at command more technical skill than the Hausaman.

A Nigerian company on parade would have struck a military observer as being composed of robust-looking soldiers of above the average height of British troops. Some of them, true, would be smallish, thickset men with heavy limbs, but many more tall with delicately sculptured heads and narrow eyes that slanted upwards at the corners – presumably an adaptation to life in semi-desert country under a brutal sun – and cheeks scarred or otherwise decorated with symmetrical incisions or tattoos, insignia varying in design from tribe to tribe. The great blue tattooed swellings on the faces of Tivs could only be described as bizarre, these 'Munchis', as the Hausaman called them, not to Western eyes handsome even as nature had constructed their features. The soldiers adopted closely shaven heads, sometimes leaving patches of short hair neatly arranged on either side of the skull; moustaches were popular among those able to produce more than a couple of dozen hairs a side and privileged senior sergeants grew short beards. Since beards were the prerogative of age and wisdom, no young fellow would be presumptuous enough to attempt one.

A number of soldiers looked jet-black, almost purple, their skins bearing a kind of bloom, like a hothouse grape; others were brown as their rifle butts and one or two very light-complexioned. Of whatever tint his skin might be, none showed the least self-consciousness of the work of Allah's paint brush and one and all spoke of themselves as 'black men'. (At that period in the dismal history of race relations, to call an American negro a 'black man' would have been resented as deeply insulting, almost as unpardonable as to call him 'nigger' or 'coon'.) I should mention that in Nigeria no official colour bar existed, nor were European settlers permitted: unlike Kenya or Rhodesia, West Africa was never regarded as 'white man's country'.

The men of B Company represented many northern tribes and districts: Kabbans and Kabbalis from French territory on the edge of the Sahara and Lake Chad; Dakkakeri pagans from Zuru (who made outstandingly good soldiers); village Fulani from the Adamawa wilds; Maiduguri Sarahs; Tivs – already mentioned – of the Benue river district; cheerful, worldly Hausamen from the old trading cities of the northern Emirates, from Kano and Katsina, from Sokoto, Zaria and Bauchi. (The names are music, they sing to me still.) The soldiers' patronymics were as limited in number as

Welsh surnames and the many Alis, Sules, Garabas, Mommans and Abdullais might have caused confusion. For distinguishing purposes, therefore, each soldier would be referred to by two names, the second being that of his native town or district. 'Usuman Gwandu', for example, denoted Usuman from Gwandu, this sensible system giving one a good idea of tribal background at a glance. As our few Southerner riflemen had only got themselves accepted by enlisting in some northern district, it couldn't be positively certain that a man whose second name was, say, Kano, hailed from that city by birth, but in nine cases out of ten he did.

Unlike men of the old Indian Army regiments, Nigerian regular soldiers inherited no father-to-son military tradition – with the British Protectorate barely thirty years established there had been no time to create one – and while grandfathers might still pride themselves on their old fighting prowess the Pax Britannica had silenced the war drum and rusted the spear. Young enlisted soldiers tended not to be of overtly martial spirit.

Unsophisticated and unlettered Nigerians were apt to be regarded as 'childish' by many a well-disposed white man because their attitudes and reactions differed from his. A child parades an active sense of curiosity, of wonder, feels no need to disguise emotions, is subject to rapid changes of mood and given more to laughter and tears than adults – white adults, that is – all hand in hand with a direct and disarming simplicity. To this extent my soldiers could indeed be considered childish: they showed such traits. Were it not for our repressive upbringing, the pressures that constantly bear upon us, the necessity of concealing or dissimulating our real feelings in order to survive in an over-complex society, we ourselves would exhibit characteristics as 'childish' as those of any African from a bush village. That we do so no longer is not gain but loss, a matter not for pride but for shame; it is we who ought to weep for our vanished spontaneity and forgotten innocence. Since the young black recruits, heirs to local cultures totally different from our own, had seen nothing of even the fringes of western civilisation before enlistment, their reactions to novelties were like those of Western children, unpredictable and frequently amusing. However transparent their feelings or ingenuous their attitudes might be, our African soldiers were nevertheless not children but men: men fortunate enough to have retained intact the spontaneity and unselfconscious sense of wonder that white adults have lost. It was as well to bear this in mind.

Crimson fez and cummerbund, yellow-bordered scarlet monkey jacket and other splendours of peacetime ceremonial dress had given way to khaki drill of the sandy tropical shade. The upper garment, a blouse with black palm-tree buttons, practical and not unbecoming, allowed no scope for criticism; it was the nether garments, worn too by British officers and NCOs during military exercises, that offended. The brain-child of General Giffard, a veteran of German East Africa during the First War, they were called 'long shorts', and unhappily for us the General persuaded the War Office (which by now had taken over responsibility for the West African forces) to approve their issue. Long shorts finished half-way up the calf, the intention, a praiseworthy one, being to protect the knees from bush thorns while allowing more air to circulate than long trousers permitted. In theory all very well, in practice long shorts not only looked undignified and ridiculous but felt distinctly uncomfortable. What the black man thought I never enquired, but we Europeans hated them. For the African soldier one concession to pre-war elegance remained in the shape of the hairy green fez with bobble on top known, rather oddly, as a 'Kilmarnock cap' – surely a far cry from any variety of Scots headgear ancient or modern. The Nigerians, who would first plaster the felt with a smelly, bottle-green gum and then brush the sticky hairs in a clockwise direction so that they lay flat, felt proud of these. No silk topper could have been more lovingly tended.

Until 1941 the soldiers wore no boots. They kept their feet clean and lightly oiled, like their rifle bolts, and painted toenails a delicate shade of red. Sandals used to be worn by the men only when out in the bush, but the War Office, soon after taking over, decided that West African troops must be made to train and march in boots in civilized style and had a consignment specially manufactured for the purpose. Some enterprising official having observed that African feet tended to be broad, the boots first provided not only looked twice the width of the standard pattern but had strongly curved sides. They resembled little boats. The soldiers, however, expressed delight; regardless of foot sizes, the bigger the boots they could get hold of the more valued would they be.

'Ali Gwombe, these boots must be far too large for you!'

'Lord, indeed they are not, truly. They are just right – little boots are no good at all. I got these fine ones from Colour Sergie Shar himself!'

Shaw, a tall regular, dour, sardonic and enterprising in several directions, a man of few words but mordant wit, was my British quartermaster sergeant, a capable and loyal man with whom I remain in touch.

As often as not a marching soldier would remove his new footwear at the first opportunity, tie the boots round his neck by their laces and continue in greater comfort with bare feet. But, like all, the passion for enormous boots cooled. A few months later the trend reversed itself; soldiers considered it chic to wear none but the smallest sizes available. Many a man would squeeze his feet into what, comparatively speaking, looked to be the daintiest of boots, stifling groans of pain as he hobbled off to flaunt them before friends. Finally the boat-like footwear came to be withdrawn, the standard British army boot took its place and the African troops learnt that it was best after all to wear those that fitted.

B Company lived in little round mud huts with thatched roofs – one man to each – laid out in the mathematically straight rows long cherished by the military mind. To help wash, starch and iron uniforms and clean and polish equipment men employed children called 'barracki boys' who for a few pence did most of the work, one little boy being shared between half a dozen soldiers. Before the outbreak of war the soldiers' wives and families had lived with them – it must have been a tight squeeze – and cooked their meals, for which the soldiers had received a cash 'subsistence allowance'. The senior wife, wearing a sergeant's red sash to underline her authority, had ruled the henroost in termagant style, wifely misdemeanours she felt herself incapable of coping with being reported to the company commander, though how he had dealt with them I can't imagine.

These sensible arrangements collapsed like the walls of Jericho as soon as the trumpets sounded for war. War demanded sacrifices; therefore a West African Army Service Corps was hastily assembled that soldier cooks might produce cook-house meals from the rations delivered to them and wives and concubines be given notice to quit. Naturally they moved no further than the nearest township and stealthily returned to their men after dark. But the authorities, having made these other arrangements, decreed it a military offence for a man to sleep in his hut with his wife, and periodically our colonel would order his company commanders to make a nocturnal search for the women whose fidelity outraged military headquarters in Lagos. Not relishing the role of peeping tom thrust upon me, I would drag my steps as, coughing or singing loudly, I approached the company lines. Shadowy female figures would always be discerned stealing mouse-like through the cactus hedge surrounding the huts when they or their men detected my noisy advent, and a perfunctory search reveal husbands snoring in celibate decorum. Though not, perhaps, all.

'Sergeant Abu Katsina? Are you there?'

'Yes indeed, sir, I am. Evening greetings to you.'

'Evening greetings to you also. You are alone?'

'It is so, certainly. But I beg you not to come in, lord. My hut is not fit for your inspection, as it will be on Saturday morning. I should feel ashamed.'

All right, Sergie Abu, I understand. Until tomorrow.'

'Until tomorrow, sir.'

And I would walk away, smiling into the darkness. Sometimes through hut doors faint feminine squeaks might be heard, sounds instantly to be suppressed by deeper voices.

Women, while despised as persons, were of importance to the black soldiers, to make love as essential and matter-of-fact to them as to eat or drink; to be a week without a woman hardship and the young men thoroughly promiscuous. With two battalions on hand, the Kaduna whores must have done well.

One left the men to their own devices after work except on Saturday mornings, when one carried out formal inspections of their living quarters, hut doors in the lines having to be wide open with the tenants standing smartly to attention on the threshold. Interiors would be so neat and spotless that one couldn't believe the huts were ever lived in.

Before I began to promote the best of my young war-enlisted men my black NCOs had all been regulars or recalled reservists, some rather too advanced in years for strenuous activity. Under the British eye these corporals and sergeants held their men in the hollow of their hands – the closer observed the more fiercely did they shout – but this admirable control was apt not to extend beyond the confines of parade ground or musketry range. In the lines, where the neat huts stood dressed by the right, the gradations of the military hierarchy would be half-forgotten and the company splinter into tribal groups, the senior member, by age or antecedents, paramount then regardless of army rank. Military policy, in this instance wisely, frowned upon the idea of platoons or companies being formed from single or closely allied tribes; rivalry might have exceeded bounds and developed into inter-tribal war.

Instead, men in the ranks were mixed together like assorted biscuits in a tin.

The Africans enjoyed being soldiers. They seemed to welcome rather than resent the strict regime I believed in imposing, striving to master the mechanical intricacies of weapons and listening attentively to what one had to say. 'Old soldier' tricks to avoid disagreeable chores were never resorted to, and none would think of reporting sick unless forced to by grave illness or disability. One might observe groups of recruits practising rifle drill in their spare time, going through the movements over and over again until satisfied with their performance. Emotional, subject to quicksilver changes of mood, the Nigerian possessed a strong sense of fun and if solemn enough on duty, off parade would constantly be laughing and joking. Our men didn't regard us as usurpers or in any way resent our presence; they hadn't yet been taught to by their politicians. Loyal, devoted to those who really liked and looked after them, the Africans knew that we belonged to a tribe far more powerful than any to be found in Nigeria. Martians we might be, but not gods.

Deep within these black men, on the surface so easily read, there lay half-buried and intangible quality, an essence alien to the minds of their white over-lords, a human strangeness reflecting elemental differences of attitude, as though the sources whence the Nigerians had sprung were bedrock, infinitely more ancient and remote than ours. We Europeans exercising paramount power seemed by comparison to live restlessly and rootless on the surface of a synthetic world, one newer than theirs and forever changing. Well-meaning persons given to repeating foolish clichés to the effect that blacks, colour apart, are just the same as whites make no allowance for human diversity, unable – perhaps unwilling – to concede that men of differing races may feel and think and act differently also.

# CHAPTER 3
## Life in Kaduna

Kaduna itself, not a natural growth, had little to recommend it. Near no old city, part of no Emirate, it suggested what in fact it happened to be, an artificial government centre planted on soil that until the British arrival had nurtured nothing more pretentious than a pagan village. The Chief Commissioner of the Northern Provinces lived in a large house surrounded by acres of parched grass supposed, one imagined, to represent a park, over his roof waving the Union Jack and black policemen in blue and scarlet uniforms barring access to unauthorised persons. Kaduna was the epitome of British stations abroad. It echoed Rawalpindi and Dar-es-Salaam, Rangoon and Colombo: the ingredients of the imperial recipe varied little. Here were the petty snobberies and assumptions of gentility, the talk of Home, the clothes no longer quite in fashion; here too the neat bungalows (their regimented gardens garish with zinnias), the boozy private parties, the European club with its Saturday night dances to music from six or seven records played over and over again. Smaller, more remote, Kaduna shared common features with Poona.

In the early days I lived in a bungalow occupied by an officer of the 5th, an entertaining and wide-awake chap called Oldfield, before the war an employee of one of those British trading octopuses with tentacles spread all over West Africa. Hard-drinking and restless, he had recently divorced his wife and regularly told me about this misadventure over our evening whisky and soda.

'She was a lovely girl. We got on fine, Charles, and gave the best parties in Calabar. She liked a drink and so do I, as you know. I was making quite a bit of money, too. Then along comes this fellow Jenkins – small, quiet, dark little sod. I never knew anything was going wrong. Of course we quarrelled a bit, but who doesn't? Have another drink?'

I would have another drink and watch the gecko lizards patrolling the cracked walls.

'Well, one day she suddenly pissed off, just like that. Vanished, skidaddled. What she saw in him God only knows. I was hellish fond of her.'

And Oldfield would look angry and indignant, finding it an effort to acknowledge that his wife had dared to prefer another man. To console himself for her defection he kept a strongly-built African woman.

'Come in, you great lump of black ivory, and have a drink! Fill my glass, too. Here's Captain Carfrae longing to see you, you great big beautiful doll!' Oldfield used to shout.

His woman, sidling in, would rock with gentle laughter, showing all her powerful white teeth. She had a soft, crooning voice and ended many English words with a musical, long-drawn-out, very pleasing Yoruba O sound. Invariably we addressed each other as 'Mr Frog-O' and 'Mrs Frog-O', though I cannot remember how this came about.

'Oh, Mr Frog-O, hullo Mr Frog-O! Dis Mr Oldfield, my master, be bad man too much-O! I no agree stay long time for him!'

And she would burst into loud laughter, peal upon peal, her ample breasts shaking.

That Oldfield should keep a black mistress was nothing out of the ordinary. Among men who had spent years in Southern Nigeria – 'Old Coasters', they called themselves – it remained common practice, just as it had been for British officials in India to maintain Hindu or Moslem ladies until in Victorian times the bustling arrival of their memsahibs put a stop to it. Well-developed young women from certain coastal tribes, if too dark for some tastes, had their admirers, but Fulanis from the northern bush were prized above all. Honey-coloured, with straight noses, antelope eyes and conspicuous grace of movement, nomads who like gypsies felt ill at ease under a roof, Fulani girls seldom became genuinely attached to Europeans and having saved a little money would forsake their lovers and vanish.

Not many young army officers shared beds with Nigerian women, but if the latter happened to be Hausa speakers cohabitation could prove a wonderful aid to learning the language quickly. African girls – even Fulanis – shy, bashful and inclined to giggle, failed to appeal to every European as objects of desire; moreover there existed a substantial risk of the venereal disease prevalent in Nigeria. Most of the soldiers contracted it in one form or another, though it produced precious little effect upon their activities. The Hausa words for gonorrhoea and a common cold are the same.

B Company second-in-command, to whom I owed many a debt, remained with me for a year. Duggy Pott, one of the officers lent to the army by the Colonial Service, was tall and strong and with a certain nobility of feature, horn-rimmed glasses giving him a scholastic air that belied considerable practical ability. Having a more than professional interest in anthropology, he taught me something of the northern tribes: their various social organisations and affiliations, initiation ceremonies and tabus. Until I picked up enough Hausa he also acted as interpreter, which must have been a trying task. Without Duggy as admirable mentor I would at first have floundered in my ignorance of local military custom and made serious mistakes. Indeed within a fortnight of taking over the company I had occasion officially to punish one of my black soldiers and was astounded when soon after he had been marched out of the office the man walked in again by himself, saluted and said in Hausa, 'I thank you, sir.' What damned impertinence! But Duggy Pott explained that what I had taken for unpardonable insubordination was no more than polite and formal acknowledgement of wrongdoing.

Jack Symons, another from the Colonial Service, unlike Duggy – a natural soldier disappointed to be recalled to Nigerian administrative duties before seeing action – had no patience whatever with military life and found the rigmarole of formal discipline and what he described as 'subservience' irritating beyond measure. Fond of Jack, I felt secretly relieved that he never became a B Company officer. A little older than myself, more sophisticated, more a man of the world and a pronounced Francophile, Jack had a delightful sense of humour and used to poke mild fun at the more extraverted Duggy Pott, at the public school accent with which he spoke Hausa and his liking for large dogs. I bowed to Jack's superior intelligence, though not too low.

The 10th Battalion officers' mess, a dreary enough place, looked more like a canteen and indeed was used as bar and restaurant rather than club. We possessed no evening uniforms to change into, nor any of the creature comforts of more civilized communal living; there were neither trophies on the wall nor regimental band to criticise. Though drinking was the rule the boozers remained morose; one had the impression that they sought oblivion rather than good cheer and swallowed alcohol as hypochondriacs swallow medicine, topers who ignored one another as far as was possible in daylight becoming boon companions after the sun had sunk, temporarily united by common affection for the gin bottle. Not a heavy drinker myself, I avoided such sessions when possible, the sound of my Yorkshire subaltern and his pals roaring out 'Nellie Dean' off key more than I could bear, sound officer and likeable man though Bill was.

On Sunday mornings Duggy and I would search for game animals to shoot, walking for miles. No lions, no elephant or buffalo existed anywhere near Kaduna, indeed little game of any description; roan antelope, tall as race-horses, easily the most impressive animals to be found locally. In the course of every expedition one or other of us saw roan slots or droppings but in the flesh the beasts remained elusive, the chance of coming across one of the small, alert troops scattered throughout thousands of square miles of orchard bush remote as that of finding the proverbial needle in its haystack. We managed to shoot occasional kob – handsome, medium-sized antelope with a chestnut coat – and also small, slinking creatures such as oribi, duiker or pale-flecked bushbuck, all hard to discern amongst the small trees and withered grass unless betraying their presence by flick of ear or flirt of tail. Sometimes a reed buck bounded away over the tussocks, his stern waving in farewell like a white handkerchief.

Our habit was to cycle ten miles towards Zaria in the chill of darkness, meet our two African hunter-guides at a pre-arranged spot by the roadside and then separate. Mijinyawa, king of the local hunters, I came to know well when I had mastered a little Hausa. He had an innocent, round face, big and melting eyes with long lashes, like a girl's, and a perpetual smile. Every local inhabitant was Mijinyawa's friend, the pagan women living in bush villages bursting into delighted whoops of high-pitched laughter as soon as they glimpsed the old trilby, presented by some satisfied client, that he wore at a devil-may-care slant and was never seen without. Mijinyawa knew the bush as intimately as we know our gardens, his alert and roving eye missing little. My refusal to shoot at waterbuck, animals Duggy told me were uncommon in the district and therefore to be spared, constantly upset him and he would reproach me bitterly. As to every Nigerian, rural or urban, a wild animal to Mijinyawa meant a walking hunk of meat; and if roan stood as high as horses waterbuck might be considered at least donkey-sized.

At daybreak the bush lay breathless. The sun, rising blood-red between stunted trees, slowly dispersed the dew delicately pricking out in tiny silver droplets the spiders' webs that garlanded every leaf and tussock; the air smelt honey-sweet, the springing new grass blanketing recently swaled patches of earth looked as green as an

Irish pasture. On and on we would trek, very circumspectly, pausing every few steps to peer and listen, until shadows grew short and the sun's heat pounded us.

Many inhabitants of Northern Nigeria spoke Hausa as their mother tongue. Pagans from remote villages who had known little of the language before enlistment soon picked up a rough-and-ready version in the lines, though it was quite common for a Nigerian soldier to have been bilingual before joining up. Without some knowledge of Hausa one had no hope of becoming an influential commander, by which I mean one who could impart ideas directly to his men instead of through an intermediary. There are people who pick up a foreign language as effortlessly as a dropped coin, but it is no accomplishment of mine and I made heavy weather of the business. Our Colonial Service officers were required to provide compulsory morning lessons for all the British, and to supplement them I employed, every evening, a sad-eyed Hausa '*mallam*', or teacher, who would shuffle into the bungalow wearing dirty robes and a fez perched askew. For months I persevered, to be gratified by the mallam's smile and well-simulated enthusiasm when, according to him, some progress had been made. 'My lord now knows much Hausa,' he would murmur falsely, his eye on my cigarette case. In four months I was able to deliver simple, halting and ungrammatical lectures to the company, every month thereafter knowledge increasing until in a year I had become reasonably fluent in Hausa of the 'barracki' sort, capable of speaking it as least as well as many Tivs.

Nigerian soldiers responded well to rhetoric, exhortation or indeed abuse. The spoken word, painted in strong colours and with a sympathetic feeling for the audience, made a mark: oratory achieved visible results. Though speechmaking may have revealed some vein of exhibitionism at other times hidden even from myself, when my Hausa was up to it I loved to gain and hold the troops' attention and watch their expressive faces. It was a joy to command men so malleable, so willing to please.

Muslim and pagan alike superstitious to a degree, the soldiers were always to be impressed by anything smelling of magic and dangerously susceptible to auto-suggestion, capable, in extreme circumstances, of willing or resigning themselves to die. One found it deeply disturbing that a healthy man, laughing and vital, might be lying dead within the week, convinced – as he might well become – that there remained no better chance of escape for him than for

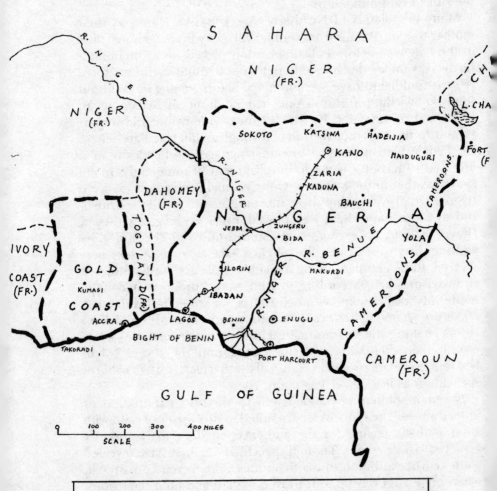

SKETCH MAP OF NIGERIA & ADJACENT TERRITORIES 1940

Orestes pursued by the Furies. A Nigerian might turn his face to the hut wall and await death under the spell of some malignant and powerful Ju-ju against which no prophylactic existed; another, taken ill and alarmed by his symptoms, might sink into despair, persuading himself that since death must inevitably follow, to fight against it was useless. A soldier unable to raise cash enough to buy the sacrificial black goat upon which, or so he told me, his life depended, died within a few days. It was my fault; I hadn't believed him. Whether the African death-wish implied exceptional powers of psyche over corporeal being, or whether the ease with which death might be wooed showed, despite appearances, a more tenuous hold on life than ours, was difficult to tell. Europeans hate to die; we fear death more, and even at an advanced age cling on grimly, the instinct of self-preservation the last to loose its hold. Only when pressed beyond endurance do we commit suicide by means more or less violent. The unsophisticated African felt no need to take so radical a step. He lay down quietly, invoked death and death came.

Most of B Company professed themselves Muslims, religious holidays always scrupulously observed and the name of Allah constantly on their lips. Indeed Allah's name would as often be invoked by those black soldiers not of the Faith as by genuine Believers. Fortune's smile was Allah's, her frown too the result of his intervention; he was assumed as capable of diverting bullets from the targets on the range as of bestowing a fine wife. In the company ranks stood also a number of pagans who, so one imagined, bowed down to wood and stone, looked to stars or sun or ancestral spirits, beliefs which seemed not to weigh too heavily upon them. The little Christian minority of various persuasions, indoctrinated at mission schools, practised a genuine if wooden faith, worshipping the white man's God with a devotion and assiduity somewhat less conspicuous in Europeans Christian by inheritance.

After some weeks I left the bungalow shared with Oldfield and his 'Mrs Frog-O' and set up house in one of my own with two rooms and huts behind it for servants. As personal 'boy' I employed Christopher, a big, handsome fellow from Benin in the South, who besides having a fair command of English turned out to be the practising Christian his name suggested.

At six o'clock in the morning he waked me daily with a cup of tea. Not by nature an early riser, I would have to force myself out of bed, shave and dress quickly, mount my old black bicycle and ride a mile down the road to the company office. The morning's first parade would be physical training or drill, enjoyed impartially by my command. At drill, called 'dancing' in Hausa, the B Company Africans really excelled, their natural sense of rhythm, of precise timing, greatly to their advantage. Ever since Sandhurst days I had taken more pleasure than most soldiers in drill well performed. My heart used to fill with pride as I yelled words of command, felt the men's immediate emotional response and saw the flash of a hundred bayonets moving as one.

When the sun had climbed above the horizon and cleared the level tops of the bush trees the air became warmer and the sky changed from grey to a delicate, translucent blue. My regular dawn depression would lift and watching the black troops at bayonet practice, seeing them leap and stab and grunt, I would feel that training so brutal desecrated the early morning calm. An hour ago these bayonets had been toys giving colour and sparkle to arms drill; now they were being handled as in battle. The Africans used to grin as they thrust their blades deep into sawdust dummies. Did they smile because it was a game, or did they see before them a helpless, an already vanquished foe?

First parade after breakfast was also the hour fixed for 'Company Office'; the time, that is, when one heard charges against defaulters or granted interviews, procedure exactly as in a British regiment except for the presence of two sergeant-majors rather than one.

'Well, Sergeant-Major, what have we got?' I might ask.

'Nothing much, sir.' Magill, an Ulsterman, at this point always took off his hat and scratched his bushy grey hair. Short and wiry with a thin red face, active, painstaking and a good warrant officer, Magill proved as great an asset as Colour Sergeant Shaw. Though he was severe with the Africans they loved their white sergeant-major dearly and on the sly would reproduce to perfection his admonitory shouts.

'Labo's charged three men with being idle on drill this morning. Didn't see much wrong myself, sir. Company looked good. They're outside now. Shall I march them in, sir, when Annang's finished typing the charge sheets?'

Sergeant Major Labo Kontagora, ready to give his evidence, would come in when called. A talkative, good-natured and fatherly old fellow, one suspected he might occasionally take bribes, his air of conscious rectitude too good to be true. Putting on my hat, I would strive to assume my most pompous and solemn manner, searching the face of each man charged, like St Peter at the gate sorting sheep from goats.

'Sule Zaria, Abdullai Yerwa, Momman Sokoto. All charged with being idle on this morning's drill parade. Evidence, Sergeant-Major?'

Labo always delivered his evidence in a slow, clear and portentous voice. By the time he finished the 'accused' might be visibly agitated, their expressions assuming a calculated combination of astonishment and innocence.

'Well,' I would ask each in turn when Labo had finished, 'what have you to say for yourself?'

'Sir, there is undoubtedly some mistake, the man observed to have been lazy cannot have been me. Allah is my witness that I was drilling excellently, as always!'

'There was a stone under my foot, sir. I did but stumble for an instant.'

'And you, Momman?'

'Ali, on my right, pushed me, sir. He is an evil fellow, that Hausaman. Also he owes me three shillings and fourpence. . . .'

The most disconcerting cases I had to deal with took the form, officially, of 'absence without leave'; on four if not five occasions men considered trustworthy disappeared completely for a matter of days. It was 'Iska', the wind, according to the African sergeant-major, who had spirited them away! Labo claimed to be able to recognise genuine Iska victims as distinct from those led astray less unwillingly by Bacchus. Though questioning closely those who, like True Thomas to the Queen of Elfland or the Knight-at-Arms to La Belle Dame, had apparently been held in thrall, I got nowhere. The men would return to the company lines exhausted, dishevelled and hungry after wandering aimlessly in the bush for a matter of days. Except for their conviction that it had been caused by Iska, the sufferers could give no explanation for their absence and appeared as bewildered as myself. One man, even two, smitten with amnesia one might credit; four or five seemed to stretch the bounds of plausibility. I neither punished these soldiers nor solved the mystery.

It was seldom that any soldier, guilty or not, resented punishment; rarer still for him to bear a grudge. But one man, Ali Gussau, a company cook, found himself sentenced by the Colonel to a stiff term of imprisonment. What the charge was I forget, though it must have been serious for me to have remanded the case for the com-

manding officer's judgement. Perhaps it was selling rations. After a
week or two of incarceration, a black prisoner might find it difficult
to remember for what crime his officers had locked him up and suc-
ceed in convincing himself that he had been innocent of any. This
happened to be the case with my cook. On his release he asked to
see me and Labo Kontagora marched him into the office. Ali
Gussau told me, in forceful language, that he had been wrongfully
imprisoned; it was my fault and he intended vigorous revenge. Dis-
concerted, I wondered what I ought to do, and to gain time decided
on a light approach. To settle the matter, I suggested, why shouldn't
we arm ourselves with a rifle and ten rounds each, lie two hundred
yards apart and take pot shots at each other? After scowling at me
for a moment, digesting this, Ali suddenly burst into uproarious
laughter, slapping his thighs. Sergeant Major Labo looked scan-
dalised. Oh no, said the cook, not a good idea; he couldn't agree to
it! And now he came to consider the matter again, he wouldn't press
his revenge after all. Still laughing, the man saluted and the
sergeant-major marched him away. I was known to be a
marksman.

One morning there occurred an odd, fortunately isolated incident. Whilst sitting quietly by myself in the company office, deep in
paper-work, I was disturbed by a corporal suddenly bursting in
without the official escort, quite beside himself with agitation and
shaking from head to toe.

'They are saying that I make love with certain of the men around
me!' he shouted repeatedly.

The Hausa words sounded more graphic than this. After a while
I managed to calm the man, assuring him I credited no such thing
and telling him to pay no attention to malicious talk. Thinking it
unwise to delve into the matter I refrained from questioning the
corporal's accusers or even asking him their names, hoping that
nothing more would be heard of this. Nothing was.

During the afternoon I might give a lecture on the progress of the
war, which I did every fortnight or so as a part-educational, part-
propaganda exercise, cunningly emphasising victories, such as
were reported, and dismissing the most comprehensive of defeats
as local setbacks. The men of B Company would sit huddled
together in patches of shade under a clump of trees near the parade
ground, their dark faces, crowned by green Kilmarnock caps,
reminding one of chocolates in a box. From the closely-packed
bodies arose the familiar, pungent odour of black humanity, musky

yet acrid, that I found not unpleasant.

Drawing rough sketch maps on a blackboard, I would attempt to explain the geography of a world unknown.

'This is where the Germans live. Here is Italy, there France and . . .'

Smiles and pointed fingers. Ah yes, 'Frenchies'; a number of men came from Chad or Fort Lamy and some could speak a few French words. But as my voice droned on and on into the stillness of the afternoon it became more and more difficult for the Africans to concentrate. They had taken plenty of exercise all morning and now they dozed. Every so often, usually when I had arrived at a vital point and was searching for an intelligible Hausa translation of thought, old Labo would bawl 'You! You're asleep! Stand up!' The African sergeant-major found it less taxing to unmask dozing soldiers than to listen to his company commander.

Lessons not too strenuous completed the military day. Tired by this time, I would watch the non-commissioned officers instruct. Always fonder of talk than of demonstration, they kept up a continuous flow of advice, encouragement and threat.

'Abu Makurdi, you are certainly a man of the bush! Where is your head? Hurry now, for the sake of Allah!'

'The master is observing you, Garaba Gwandu. Do not, I entreat you, throw away my trust.'

'Excellent, Mohamman, very good indeed. Perhaps one day you will become the owner of a stripe . . .'

Creating young non-commissioned officers made me feel like the Pope presenting Cardinal's hats. The newly-elevated lance-corporals, stunned with joy, would for the first days of grandeur be so afraid their golden stripes might be spirited away by some Ju-ju that they could hardly bear to take eyes from arms.

When at the end of a day's work I cycled wearily up the red laterite road to the peace of the bungalow Christopher, sympathetic, would pull off my boots and socks and bring tea. The problems of days to come would for a space be forgotten, my soldier's armour thankfully discarded.

The kittens playing by my feet reminded me of the cosy English domestic world of firesides and women's voices. I would picture my parents in the drawing room at home, wireless tuned in ready for the next news bulletin, frost white on the lawn – in the tropics one becomes attracted to Christmas card images – and for the hundredth time ask myself why on earth I had volunteered to serve in a

West African backwater where nothing of importance could ever happen. As a regular officer, I ought to be closer to action. To prepare black soldiers a thousand miles from the nearest battlefront to meet some contingency so remote that no one guessed what form it might take – whether indeed it would ever arise – struck me as negative indeed. Certainly it was hard work, ten times harder than it must have been in the old polo-playing days, but that I didn't mind. What frustrated me was having no clear aim, no star to follow. Military friends outside India, if not yet in action somewhere or other, would in North Africa or the United Kingdom be training themselves and their men to fight Germans or Italians. And in Britain one could get weekend leave in which to visit families and girls and sit by drawing room fires.

I worked long hours – unnecessarily long – an unconscious motive, no doubt, being to achieve some degree of physical exhaustion, evenings holding out no prospect of entertainment unless to be spent solemnly drinking in the mess. Losing all sense of proportion, I would examine past pleasures under a magnifying glass, to see minor flirtations enlarging themselves into major passions and distant girls becoming infinitely desirable now that there was none, or none white, to take their place, and would write pages of rubbish to perfectly ordinary young women transmuted by imagination into miracles of grace and beauty. The recipients must have been surprised.

# CHAPTER 4

# Excursions to the Bush

Under orders to construct a training base from local resources near a village called Kachia, in April 1941 I took B Company ninety miles south-east into the heart of the bush, the rest of the battalion to join us when the huts we were to build should be ready for occupation. As soon as our train was puffing southward from the Kaduna siding I began to feel joyfully free. Released from barrack chains, I became in imagination a Nigerian expedition's leader, a twentieth-century Mungo Park, a Chatterton or Landon. It happened to be the birthday of my youngest platoon commander and the company officers laughed and sang, sucked oranges and sprawled about in their compartments like pre-war Saturday afternoon trippers on their way to the seaside. The Africans, less happy, preferred the dirty Kaduna streets, the palmwine and the brothels; but they had known their destination in advance and within a week the female population of Kachia was to show a startling rise. Miles of orchard bush trooped past the carriage windows in steady green monotony until at a wayside halt we clambered out of the train, collected baggage, formed up in the dust of the station yard and began the march of fifteen miles which separated railway halt from camp-site, the Africans roaring the usual choruses, their singing as automatic as the tramp of boots, the shouted words as uninhibited as melodies were heart-stirring. Before we had covered six miles the sky began to darken, thunder boomed like heavy guns and big raindrops made worm-casts in the dust. In a minute the rain came pelting down, khaki blouses and those wretched long shorts clinging to our skins, water collecting in the wide brims of bush hats. Lightning flashed blue, the tree-tops a sickly green against the thunder clouds; the country became wilder and more hilly. We passed two villages and glimpsed fat naked Pagan women, like seals, peering from mud huts.

Dusk fell before we had reached our destination and we halted in the bush, the thunder storm drifting to the west. The troops collected wood and managed to make great fires under the trees, Duggy Pott put a record on his gramophone and somebody produced a bottle of whisky. In fifteen or twenty minutes our uniforms were bone dry.

Next morning Duggy and I visited the Kachia Headman, an elderly Hausa speaker with a grey goatee beard.

'Greetings, greetings of the morning,' we said.

'What news have you?' he enquired. It was a set formula.

'There is no particular news.'

'Indeed. You are keeping well?'

'We are. And you? We trust your people are in good health? Your crops flourishing?'

'All well, O Lord, thanks be to Allah. And your soldiers?'

'In good spirits.'

'Splendid. God bless you. May your lives be long.'

After these obligatory but meaningless politenesses had been exchanged we came to the purpose of our visit and inquired whether building materials were ready.

'Lord, my labourers are few – little bamboo has yet been cut. But grass mats have been woven,' said the Headman.

We received from him that evening the usual gift of eggs and skinny chickens, returning the honours in coin, as dictated by custom; and also buying in Kachia two cows for the company to feast on. The sight of plentiful meat on the hoof was loudly acclaimed and Sergeant-Major Labo Kontagora came up and saluted.

'Sir, it is fitting that we celebrate and arrange dances. We are much pleased,' announced Labo.

The cows to be sacrificed were seized by the legs, thrown to the grass and held down by a dozen men while others, acting with horrible, grinning deliberation, began in the prescribed Muslim manner to sever the beasts' throats. Blood spurted over the bushes and I looked away. When the cows had at length expired their warm carcases were rapidly but carefully dismembered and every man given a ration of beef which he proceeded to cut up into generous mouthfuls, skewering each lump to a sharpened stick and thrusting it into the nearest fire.

In the afterglow of sunset the troops, who had meanwhile lit a number of bonfires in a clearing, to the accompaniment of much chatter and beating of drums began to dance. Every tribe strongly enough represented within the company had its separate bonfire, those with kin too few to form a dancing troupe of their own wandering about and watching critically, like men inspecting the stalls at a fairground, each believing his own tribe's traditional dances better than any on show at Kachia.

Tivs from the Benue river valley drew the biggest crowd, and deserved to. Thickset men with blue-tattooed faces, filed teeth and air of bovine innocence – I have mentioned them before – they were heroic now. Naked except for army blankets tucked about their bellies, the Tivs stamped singing round their blazing bonfire in a wide circle, every movement beautifully rhythmic and controlled as they turned, bowed and twisted as one man, firelight, flickering on arm and solid torso, burnishing their dark skins and causing muscles to stand out in tawny relief. Their chanting, lilting yet brutal, shouted virility; it was the bellowing of bulls. Gradually the dance movements quickened, singing became fiercer, sweat poured from heaving Tiv bodies and every man of the African spectators, surrendering to uncontrollable excitement, began to agitate his own legs and hips, jerking buttocks and snapping fingers. I too was hypnotised by the rhythm, held riveted to these posturing black men until at length, drained of vitality, they collapsed to the earth.

Half-dazed, I was making my way to my camp bed when Labo Kontagora appeared from the shadows.

'The "Munchis" were very fine,' he said. 'I saw you liked their dancing, sir. Truly it is a thing they do well.'

'But you, Labo? I didn't see you dancing?'

'Lord, here I have no "brothers". My father's home is unknown to me. He was a slave, seized and taken to Kontagora as a child. Goodnight, sir. May your life be long.'

Was his father's unfortunate history the cause of my sergeant-major's influence being something less than all-pervasive?

I felt happy at Kachia, with little paper work to do and no tiresome interference from senior officers. We enjoyed our freedom, and after sweating all day supervising the erection of grass huts would lie at ease in long chairs peacefully drinking whisky and gazing across a river valley to the line of blue hills beyond. When the rest of the battalion marched in, Kachia camp at once lost its special atmosphere. The newcomers were a crowd of brash and noisy holiday-makers invading a quiet country village, we, the residents, hating the intrusion but outnumbered and engulfed.

'See! Our Captain looks at the weather – the great Colonel is coming! See! Our Captain looks at his watch – the great Colonel is coming!' sang the B Company soldiers. There were indeed Commanding Officer's inspections; also long and tiresome battalion exercises. Finally we fought mock actions all the way back to Kaduna, averaging twenty miles a day on our feet.

In August 1941 the regular battalions of the Nigeria Regiment, after fighting victoriously in Somalia and Ethiopia at negligible cost, returned in triumph to their homeland. Because they had heard 'shots fired in anger' the officers were regarded by us as heroes and we resented our own inglorious inactivity the more. Two or three were sent to Kaduna to lecture about the campaign. We hung upon their every word: British victors at that stage of the war found themselves a novelty. Unluckily several of these talks were delivered by a man I had known at school and Sandhurst who cultivated a manner of speech so quiet as to be all but inaudible, while managing at the same time to reduce English understatement to so negative a level that one had, as it were, to read between the lines of every whispered sentence. When formal lectures and discussions were over for the day we would gather round the veterans in the mess, keeping their glasses well filled in the hope of extracting scraps of information omitted from the official talks.

'Well, old boy, to tell the honest truth it was nearly a walkover. Damned interesting and damned good fun. Drink? We carried bottles of the stuff. And those smashing Eyeti girls in Addis! Lost or mislaid their husbands one way or another, you see. Still, they had to make a living somehow . . .'

The casual words dropped like cold pebbles into the mess silence. Evidently the fruits of victory had not been bitter.

Towards the end of the year B Company went on its travels again, this time in the opposite direction. After marching north for thirty miles along the Zaria road, faces and arms coated with reddish dust, we bivouacked for ten days in the inevitable bush.

The final exercise was to be a company attack against an 'enemy-held' village. Mist still obscured the treetops as the African rank and file squatted in sleepy groups, dipping their dark hands into mess-tins full of rice, meat and red palm oil, munching in relaxed contentment as oil dripped like blood from their fingers. The sergeants, superior beings, possessed battered spoons, which they wielded as a gardener his trowel. Breakfast over, I gave last-minute instructions to Duggy Pott, in charge of the opposing force, and buckling on his equipment he made his way through the trees, walking with a characteristic and tireless slouch. Twenty Africans followed him – the 'enemy' – hatless so that they could readily be distinguished, some carrying the empty two-gallon petrol cans that when drubbed with sticks were supposed to simulate the chatter of hostile machine guns. The rest of the company jeered and hooted as the 'enemy' filed past: in face of opposition so feeble they anticipated easy victory.

'Are you Germans or Italians?' they shouted. 'Certainly if Sule there with that petrol can is firing a machine gun we shall not die today!' Sule's inaccuracy on the rifle ranges was notorious.

The Nigerians enjoyed this gentlemanly mock warfare, the knowledge that no blood would be spilled nor heads broken reassuring. They intended, when the time came, to show real dash and ferocity, but make-believe was always delightful and if they fought impressively enough the captain might allow them to sleep for the rest of the day!

A tall, idle ex-Nigerian Police officer called Godwin was to command the company for this exercise, my subaltern – he who made a habit of roaring 'Nellie Dean' out of tune – having had his turn already. For myself I intended to watch and make critical notes, to frown or smile as each situation might deserve: director, umpire and arbiter of fates rolled into one. When Godwin delivered his orders to the assembled white platoon commanders, unusual attention was accorded him. Godwin was no more than a platoon commander himself, but as their own reputations would also be at stake his peers could be relied on to do their best, even to interpreting instructions in ways more enterprising than Godwin himself might have intended. The officers looked so serious, the Africans, arrayed for battle, so determined and grim that one had to remind oneself that these fighting men, actors gesticulating against a backcloth of grass and trees, would only be rehearsing their true role.

In a compact body the company swung out from camp to the Zaria road. A crane rose from the water's edge as we crossed a bridge over the river, his wings, flashing back and white, flailing the air with ponderous strokes, his cries hoarse.

'Ah – Goraka – a good omen,' remarked some of the men. The West African crowned crane, his tuft of royal feathers standing stiffly erect, like a shaving brush, was considered a lucky bird.

The three platoons, deploying, advanced through the bush on either side of the road, khaki figures sliding in and out of sight among desiccated trees. Ahead of them scouts probed, aunt sallies for the enemy. At first, conscious of the dangers of their situation, the scouts moved too hesitantly and I made an adverse entry in my notebook. Godwin, as sensitive to criticism as most other lazy people, saw this and frowned.

After advancing for two miles without being shot at the scouts, much bolder now, acted as though altogether careless of their lives; they were finding it difficult to remain indefinitely alert and now the morning sun rose high and hot. Then, suddenly, the fight was on. The crack of blank cartridges came from the hidden village and a scout, by my order, fell writhing. Godwin, signalling to his leading platoon, waving imperiously his large brown hand, looked quite the part and soon a tremendous battle raged. Soldiers ran here and there as blank ammunition popped repeatedly; whistles shrilled; officers and sergeants yelled orders and petrol tins were drubbed. Menacing roars proved to be the war cries of the reserve platoon who, executing a flanking movement, had mistaken the direction of their enemy and charged into empty bush. When the action had been at length decided and B Company (without assistance from Godwin's reserve) awarded its predestined victory, 'enemy' bodies littered the roadside, prostrate in attitudes of terrifying realism, too-convincing parodies of death. The imperial force had also sustained casualties, if not so many, several of whom turned over into more comfortable positions to avoid sun on their faces. The men of the reserve platoon, shamefaced, smiling in embarrassment, returned without honour from their fruitless charge into the blue and my bugler sounded the 'Stand Fast', which martial blare frightened for a moment the naked little boys and girls who had come from nowhere to stare at us. The dead resurrected themselves as at the last trumpet and we took off our equipment and sat in shade, gulping warm water from felt-covered bottles.

Late in the afternoon the company marched into camp, dusty but singing loudly:

'Hit the wire [telegraph] to Kano! Those bitches of whores will be overjoyed when we come back to them . . .'

'You, tall young man, keep marching on – you, wives of gun-carriers, you keep moving too . . .'

'Allah the one God is great, and honoured be the name of his prophet Mohammed . . .'

'Look out, soldier! We are on our way to see Hitler, that stupid fellow . . .'

One man alone would chant the verses, words partly extemporised if the chanter had wit enough, while everybody joined in the chorus. This Hausa and Tiv singing was audible from far away, rising and falling cadences echoing through the bush like distant cannon. Sustained for mile after mile with heart-warming unanimity and power, the tremendous choruses, so characteristic of the Nigerian soldier and like sunlight and dust invariable elements of any march, never failed to move me. I knew every one by heart.

Before sunset Duggy and I, shadows long on the rocks, wandered over to the river to watch our men bathing. Little heaps of uniform were neatly arranged by the water's edge and in the river naked Africans shouted like boys and splashed one another, their shaven heads bobbing up and down like dark waterfowl on the muddy stream. Some sat on boulders basking in the last of the sunshine; others, standing in shallow water, rubbed themselves from head to toe with soap. Whether sitting or standing every naked man, as he always did, made strenuous efforts to hide his member between his legs, not only from Duggy Pott and me but from his fellow bathers also. To be seen exposed was considered vulgar and immodest. All such attempts were laughable; the Nigerian male is well-endowed, to say the least, and contort himself as he might the desired concealment scarcely a possibility.

# CHAPTER 5

# Polish Officers, and a Ju-Ju Story

As soon as the company had returned to Kaduna I fell ill with malaria and was sent to hospital. Rejoining the battalion after ten days' absence – taking a leaf from our book it was camping in the bush – I came across a dozen strange officers standing impatiently outside the grass hut that did duty as Orderly Room. They were Polish.

I believe it had been Churchill's idea to send Polish officers to West Africa. In Britain, apparently, no Polish Brigade or Division had yet been formed and nobody knew what to do with the officers who had managed to reach England. To send them to West Africa (out of sight and mind) may have struck the prime minister as a neat solution to the problem, but from a Polish point of view the plan was cruel and absurd. Their mission not to underwrite the British Empire but to fight Germans or Russians – ours differed as to which enemy posed the greater threat to their country – Polish officers could hardly be expected to identify themselves with a military system embracing British leaders on the one hand and black colonial troops on the other. That the Poles didn't immediately refuse to play a part in this charade, that they tried to work with us at all, reflected great credit on them.

The Poles, it must be confessed, became something of a burden to us for the first couple of months. Resenting help, eager to take offence, their outlook differed from ours. Every Pole felt intense national pride, a pride burning with so bright a flame and defended so fiercely against imagined assaults that it left him little energy to attend to military duties, the Polish eagle, a sensitive bird, constantly on the wing in quest of slights. At first mutual relations were unhappy and awkward; we felt unable to breach the wall of what we considered Polish arrogance. To some extent, indeed, our Polish officers appeared divided amongst themselves. We were given to understand that only two social classes existed in Poland: aristocrats who owned land, and the lower orders whose duty it was to serve them. Our battalion had been sent some of each, though more, I think, of the latter, who turned out to be respectable bourgeois citizens, however much despised they might be by the Polish gentlemen who in days of peace had adorned lancer regiments.

One evening in the mess, chatting to my own Polish cavalry lieutenant, I happened to say something about one of his compatriots sitting not far off.

'That officaire? He is not propaire officaire – he is ploddy peesant!'

The unhappy 'peesant' remained silent, but seemed to shrivel under the lieutenant's scowl of scorn.

Overtly critical of our military dogma, the Poles viewed British training methods with scepticism.

'Why these black men do they lie there?' I was asked the first time I took a group of Polish officers to see some exercise.

'They are supposed to be occupying a defensive position,' I said mildly.

'Defence? That ees not defence, sir. It is ploddy seely! Now in Polish army . . .'

There followed a prolonged and partly incomprehensible account of Polish defensive tactics. One hesitated to point out that the Polish Army had been cut to pieces in 1939; nor had one the right, crushed as it was between Germans on one flank and Russians on another and by tanks against which the Polish lancers, famed as cavalry throughout Europe for two hundred years, found themselves impotent at last.

When I came to know them I got on pretty well with the Poles, including B Company's subaltern, a landed Count, a young regular cynical, soft-spoken and a notable snob. If I passed muster it must have been by the skin of my teeth. Elegant and graceful with high cheekbones, slanting brown eyes and a neat little moustache, this gentleman did obey orders, but in such a manner as to inform one, more clearly than words could, that he considered our whole military edifice beneath his notice. Once I became really furious with him when in the middle of a hot and exhausting exercise he simply gave up, leaving his African platoon to fend for itself. I upbraided him so fiercely that feeling himself seriously insulted he challenged me to a duel (by which act he at least acknowledged me worthy of one). I neither accepted nor refused and half an hour later he politely apologised.

Jack Symons told me of a Pole in his company who, during a halt in the middle of some dreary twenty-mile march, pulled from his pocket a photograph of himself magnificently arrayed as a pre-war mounted officer in full dress.

'And look at me now!' he said sadly, pointing to his bush hat, creased long shorts and sweat-stained blouse.

The absence of women worried our Polish officers. One of them approached me in search of a solution.

'Most of us,' I said primly, 'wait until we go home. African women are often diseased.'

'To be without 'oman for more than one year?' he exclaimed incredulously. 'To be without 'oman for one month it is impossible!'

Most quickly found black mistresses or indulged themselves casually and – it was to be supposed – often. But not, perhaps, the fastidious Count.

The Poles liked to sing together in harmony, their national pride and bitterness of spirit finding release in music. Occasionally, to show goodwill, they gave concerts to their British comrades-in-arms and I would listen with tears in my eyes to Russian and Polish songs, imagining endless snow-streaked plains and sombre pine forests, banners and rough-hewn chivalry. Our Polish officers, compelled to serve under strangers in a foreign country with which they had nothing to do, driven from their homeland by swords too strong for them, deserved better understanding than they may have received.

After I left the 10th Battalion I met with no more Poles: there happened to be none with my new unit. But when eventually black divisions were ordered to India and Polish officers serving in them given the option of returning to Europe or remaining with their battalions, a surprising number elected to stay on and fight in Burma with the British and Africans.

My 'boy' Christopher, the Bene from the south, served me well and I grew fond of him. His manner and bearing struck me as superior, a cut above that of our other southern camp followers. One night early in 1942, as I was thinking of going to bed, in rushed the 'small boy' assistant to Christopher, a lad of about fourteen.

'Mastah come quick!' he cried. 'Christopher bad too much!'

I followed him to the two-roomed shack behind my bungalow and by the light of a paraffin lamp saw Christopher, completely unconscious, lying limply on his bed face upwards, naked to the waist, eyes open, fixed and with no more expression in them than a dead man's. He was emitting loud and indescribably appalling groans or howls at regular intervals. Not human sounds, they chilled my blood.

'Christopher! Wake up! Wake up!' I shouted, shaking him violently.

After a minute Christopher, trembling, came to himself. At first he appeared bewildered, then smiled and said he must have had a bad dream. Though he showed neither fear nor anxiety, I had never seen or heard anything like this before. It was impossible to believe that a mere nightmare could have changed Christopher into something other than human, and walking quickly to our medical officer's bungalow a hundred yards away I described what had happened. After listening good-humouredly enough the doctor, pooh-poohing my fears, produce a couple of sleeping pills. I made my boy swallow them.

'I trouble master too much. Thank you, sir,' said Christopher in his normal voice.

Telling the 'small boy' to keep eyes and ears wide open, I returned to my sitting room feeling extremely uneasy and tried to read a book. Half an hour later the lad, very frightened, ran in again and in a moment I was with Christopher. He lay as before with wide, unseeing eyes and from his throat issued those terrible sounds: it was as though the spirit of some beast possessed him. Again and again I shook him and shouted but without the least effect. Then I ran for the doctor, who by now was in bed; grumbling but losing no time he put on a dressing gown and followed me to the hut. Nothing could be heard as we approached and the doctor entered alone, after a moment reappearing at the doorway to beckon me in. Christopher still lay with his eyes open, but silent now. He was dead.

All night his woman sobbed and shrieked. She had been hiding in the other room.

The doctor, puzzled and perturbed, next morning arranged for a post mortem at the Kaduna hospital, but nothing whatever came to light. Christopher had been a healthy man in the prime of life, reported the pathologist; the cause of his death could not be ascertained.

At the funeral I learnt that to his 'brothers', meaning fellow tribesmen, Christopher's death was no surprise nor mystery; they had anticipated it. The woman he had lived with – not his wife, as I supposed her – possessed a husband far away in Benin, a notorious and formidible Ju-ju man of whom all but Christopher had been terrified. They had warned him, his 'brothers' said, that to run off with this woman would mean death, but my Christian 'boy', above such superstitious fears, had laughed at them.

I have said that Africans, strongly susceptible to auto-suggestion, were capable in certain situations of willing themselves to die. But surely it cannot have been auto-suggestion that killed Christopher. He had defied the Ju-ju man; and when shaken into his senses after the lad's first call had seemed his usual self.

Even today I find this mystery disquieting to say the least.

Deddi Mazari, a northern Hausa speaker, took Christopher's place and stayed with me until I left the Nigeria Regiment nearly three years later. Deddi was slim, black-skinned but not negroid in appearance, his features delicate, his long fingers fluttering like moths. Usually dignified, the perfect butler, he used to greet my feeblest jokes with peal upon peal of high-voiced mirth, becoming convulsed, bent double in merriment, tears of laughter still to be seen in his eyes long after the fits were over. Deddi, volatile and emotional, was made of more delicate material than the other 'boys', who finding him easy to bait and quick to anger used to tease him. Sensitive though illiterate, able to recognise the limitations of tribal ways of life, he showed perception of a quality more feminine than masculine in its sharp-pointed aptness. Had he been an educated man living under a colder sun Deddi might have made his reputation as wit. Loyalty by no means precluded him from offering advice when he felt it necessary, whether or not I asked for it; nor did Deddi remain uncritical of my conduct.

Camels, heat, black tents and sand figured, he said, in his childhood recollections. Deddi had, I surmised, been born somewhere in the Western Sahara, deep in French territory, but though several times I tried to locate 'Mazari' on a large-scale atlas Deddi's geographical sense remained vague, his home, according to himself, lying 'very near' certain villages shown on the map as hundreds of miles apart. That will-o'-the-wisp oasis could never be pinpointed. Had Deddi Tuareg blood?

On a Sunday morning, after he had been with me some months, Deddi brought a young girl along. She had a kind of wild-animal charm, her dark skin glistening, her naked breasts attractively curved.

'This is the daughter of he who mends bicycles,' said Deddi. 'I am arranging to wed her, for my present wife is barren. I seek your approval, lord.'

The girl stood bashfully in the middle of the room, her eyes fixed on the coloured raffia mat. To entertain her I put a record on Duggy's borrowed gramophone, plumping for Ravel's 'Bolero' out of the few available because its rhythm sounded as distinctive as that of an African drumbeat. The girl, forgetting her shyness and listening wide-eyed, began to sway her body. The mask of innocence slipped off and an alert, concupiscent expression took its place. 'Again!' she said as soon as the music stopped. After the fifth repetition Deddi, frowning, led her away, evidently considering that his young woman had behaved in an unbecomingly forward manner. I heard his high voice raised in anger as soon as he had closed my door.

He married her, but after a few months of connubial life dashed into my hut – we were then in Sokoto – in a state of hysterical excitement.

'I will kill her! By Allah I swear I will kill her, and him also!' he shouted, waving a knife and quite beside himself.

His grey face was wet with sweat and his eyes rolled like a stallion's. At first I could make no sense of his reiterated threats but at length, having collected the story's broken fragments and pieced them together as best I could, understood that he had caught his new wife gambolling about with the young servant of a brother officer.

'Don't be so foolish, Deddi. Probably it was nothing at all,' I said lamely. 'And if you do kill her, you yourself will be hanged from the Sokoto gallows!'

Words made no impression – Deddi, frenzied, quivering with mortally wounded pride, far beyond reason. It was like a scene from the fifth act of *Othello*. Keeping him inside the hut I sent another servant for two military policemen who, after a struggle, succeeded first in disarming and then in dragging Deddi fighting to the guard-room into preventive custody, where two days of incarceration cooled his blood. Meanwhile the youth accused, showing admirable good sense, ran away to another part of the country and enlisted.

A week passed before Deddi smiled. As far as I know he ceased to pay attentions to his wife and the poor girl either left him or was banished. It proved impossible to discover what became of her; whenever I enquired Deddi pretended not to hear.

# CHAPTER 6

# Interludes: Hadeijia and Home

The Japanese had plunged into the war: one Far Eastern disaster followed another. It became an effort to make my afternoon lectures either convincing or optimistic and I began to avoid the Africans' questions. For us, however, life went on just as usual, Japanese and Germans alike remote.

By March 1942 I anticipated leave in England, in normal circumstances due after an eighteen month West African 'tour', though in wartime a tour of duty might be anything between fifteen and twenty-four. Like all men 'end of tourish' I became irritable, listless and lazy, the grasshopper a burden. Jack Symons also expected home leave. Since there could be no means of knowing in advance the date of one's actual departure, owing to the irregularity of shipping, I was instructed to hand over B Company to a Rhodesian officer of the battalion, Captain Karlshoven, a competent man. To employ us meanwhile the brigade-major sent Jack and me to the Emirate of Hadeijia, to find and reconnoitre routes which could be used by motor transport during impending inter-brigade manoeuvres. The work involved, not onerous, in the event was to occupy us for three full days at most, but the brigade-major had generously allowed us ten.

Wearing civilian clothes to flaunt our temporary independence, Jack and I drove by turns a borrowed army truck in the back of which, under a canvas awning, sat Deddi, Jack's boy Alhamadu and our two soldier orderlies, surrounded by valises, guns, tinned food and cooking things. This was to be a carefree interlude, a preliminary taste of freedom, and we urged the truck to a reckless and lumbering speed, dust flowing out under our tyres and red, billowing blankets hanging in our wake like smoke from a steamer. As we rattled northward the green of the bush country began to fade and bleach, trees to become fewer and more thorny. Villagers parading the dry-season track laughed, waved and yelled at us and we smiled and waved back, bowing like royalty. Past beehive huts neat in the shade of mango trees, past withered maize stalks yellow in cultivated fields we clattered until we came to Zaria, bright with the scarlet blossom of flame trees. Thence on to Kano, where the

Saharan caravans halted and where outside the mud walls of the city camels stalked, the first I had seen in Nigeria. Kano, in the heart of Hausaland, was a foreign country after Kaduna, but reckoning we had little time for sight-seeing we retired early to a railway rest-house whining with mosquitoes, next morning ploughing through inches of white sand powdering like snow the route to Hadeijia. It happened to be a track we were supposed to assess and every so often we would stop to make notes or draw sketches. Twice the truck embedded itself in sand up to the axles, and though on each occasion four of us managed to free it, progress remained slow.

Having lost our way several times amid starfish confusions of broad white paths, we were overtaken by darkness with five miles still to go, our headlamps reflected dazzlingly from the glowing sand as we drove between cactus hedges down long narrow lanes of light. A home-bound peasant provided final directions; and close to a long wall guarding the Emir's harem we found a sign board indicating the district officer's house.

No other European lived in Hadeijia Emirate. The district officer, an acquaintance of Jack's, felt compelled to release a long-damned river of words: it was past midnight before we could escape from his bungalow to the rest-house allotted us. Our host, middle-aged and ruddy-cheeked, possessed a delightfully Edwardian manner of speech. He would, I imagined, have felt at home in an Ivy Compton-Burnett country house. In such an outpost as Hadeijia his clipped and courteous phrases put one in mind of the old cartoons showing dinner-jacketed empire builders sitting in state on tiny tropical islands.

Next morning Jack tried to persuade the district officer to come duck shooting with us.

'My dear fellow, it's years since I shot, positively years. Upon my word, I shan't be able to hit a thing,' he protested. 'Oh all right, if you wish. Ali, look out my cartridges. Capital sport on the lake – capital!'

Half an hour's jolt down a camel track in the army truck took us to a lake set jewel-like in a wood. Red and white waterlilies quilted its surface; three gaunt dead trees, frosty with the droppings of a thousand birds, stood sentinel in shallow water; egrets trod the mud or flapped across it like whirling snowflakes. Far out in the middle of the lake we could see clustered the dark dots of wildfowl.

We crept to our separate stands by the water's edge, hiding behind grass and clumps of reed. A company of little boys carrying

enormous chestnut-glossy gourds – they had been recruited by the
district officer from a nearby village to act as beaters – formed a line
across the far side of the lake, each straddling his gourd, and at a
given signal began to propel themselves over the water using hands
as oars, whooping, shouting and smacking the surface to scare the
duck into flight. Showers of spray sparkled in the sunlight and
ducks, vocally indignant and alarmed by the invasion, rose in
bunches of ten and twenty and with great flurry and beating of
pinions winnowed swiftly round and round, twisting and turning
with a simultaneous flash of pale undersides. There were pintail
and gadwall, pochard and garganey. Guns banged, puffs of blue
smoke drifted to the breeze; dead birds, crashing into the reeds or
plummeting to the water, were collected by our soldier orderlies –
grinning black retrievers – who plunged after them with unflagging
zest, enjoying every moment. The Kaduna barrack square seemed
as far away as England.

While Jack and I conscientiously devoted most mornings to the
plotting of local tracks and the exploration of Hadeijia, during the
sun-fierce afternoons we idled, shamefully dozing away our hours of
freedom. One evening Jack, in playful mood after several whiskies-
and-soda, thought to pull his boy's leg.

'Alhamedu! Get two women!' he said.

'Sir, I will at once,' replied Alhamedu without turning a hair.

Deddi, leering, began to giggle, and before we could prevent
them both boys had dashed out of the bungalow.

Alhamedu re-appeared in an hour, saluted his master and in the
manner of a butler announcing guests told him gravely that the
ladies had arrived.

'Bring them in.' said Jack, beginning to laugh; 'no doubt they'll
be lovely!'

Instead of the buxom young women we expected, two
frightened and pathetic-looking old crows appeared in the doorway, whispering nervously, twisting their hands together and shifting from one large bare foot to another. Alhamedu, deciding that
the joke should be against his master, must have selected them with
care. After an awkward pause the episode was closed by Jack who,
giving the women two shillings each, suggested they might wish to
return to their homes. They stared at us, unable to understand why
they should have been brought all this way for professional services
apparently unwanted; but two shillings was money and off they
shuffled, clutching the silver to bosoms like leather straps. No
sooner had the old ladies left than Deddi began to scream with

laughter. In another minute he was doubled up and quite hysterical, the impassive Alhamedu having to drag him away.

A deputation of NCOs from B Company waited upon me outside the bungalow one evening shortly after our return from Hadeijia.

'Sir, it is clear that you have left us,' said their leader, 'and perhaps are angry. We have displeased you?'

'No,' I explained, 'of course I'm not angry, but I am waiting for a ship to carry me to England for leave. That is why I have handed over the company to Captain Karlshoven.'

The Africans, listening gravely, were respectful if not reassured. I wasn't believed; my words, they thought, must be designed to conceal desertion. A silence ensued before their leader spoke again.

'The new captain is a good officer, that we already know. But the soldiers cry out for you, sir. They say "where is our master, Captain Karfuri?" and we do not know how to answer them.'

I felt very touched. These men were friends, they warmed my heart; without them life in Kaduna would have been empty. Inviting the NCOs into the house – they had been standing stiffly to attention on the gravel outside the window – I produced cigarettes and we discussed episodes in B Company's brief history: the march towards Zaria and Corporal Ali Gassol's non-stop singing; the swimmer Dan Kachia's inexplicable and sudden death in a shallow pool; the night battle with the 5th Battalion in which we had covered ourselves with glory, routing our foes and reducing them to immobility by removing valves from the tyres of every three-tonner. Then we discussed the war.

'War?' said one. 'You should have seen us, lord, in East Africa. The Italians are poor creatures, strangers of some sort. Not black like us, nor yet quite white, but pale brown and no use in battle. Why, we killed them in thousands!'

Numerical accuracy is, after all, a trifling matter and the veteran who made this speech drew murmurs of assent, heads nodding sagely.

'Yes, it is so,' said another. 'What Sergie Garaba says is true indeed. The Italians are altogether useless!'

Only three of the men present had ever seen an Italian soldier, the speaker not one of them.

'And the Germans, sir? When will they "eat defeat"?' they asked.

'Neither I nor any man can tell, but be sure they will be cast down in the end. Then there are the Japanese, you must remember, who are yellow and small and treacherous, neither black like you, brown like the Italians nor white like me – but yellow as a dying leaf!'

'Most strange! But we are finer men?'

'Of course,' I said, 'much finer.'

Somewhat mollified, the deputation left me, the last of the sunlight playing on shaven heads as they swung down the path.

In April 1942 I travelled south to Lagos by train to embark in the boat expected within a day or two. It never arrived. Weeks passed and I became bored to death. Officers waiting for leave were herded into the usual dismal transit camp and there I became friendly with a man called Royston Morley, normally a BBC producer, who had been a war correspondent in North Africa and now hoped for a passage. One evening, for want of anything better to do, we decided to explore the seamier side of Lagos, the transit camp adjutant, a red-faced, beefy man, volunteering to act as guide. He knew the ropes, he said. We didn't doubt him.

The night we chose was one swelteringly hot, every back street and alley-way stinking of goats, paraffin and excrement. A taxi-driver, who also seemed to know the ropes, dropped the three of us outside a house modestly announcing itself as 'The Nigerian Bar'. Furtively we knocked and a little boy opened the door. Floor boards creaked, dust and stench assailed. Madam, boldly painted, welcomed us warmly, as well she might; we were her only customers. We found ourselves in a room with a plush sofa, several rickety chairs and two paraffin lamps. The boy produced bottles of Congo beer. We sat silent, furtive conspirators waiting for the plot to be unfolded, and were half way through our drinks before three or four young girls entered, eyes kohl-smudged and cheeks grey with powder, pointed breasts thinly veiled by green or red taffeta, gestures tired and faces without animation. Now and again one of them would essay a smile, showing teeth that looked unnaturally white. It was impossible to feel the faintest prick of lechery; more than a couple of yellow Congo beers would have been needed for that. We avoided one another's glance, anticipation stifled and lust still-born. Madam prattled away but none listened, the heat and stink pressing tight against us like an anaesthetic. We finished our beer quickly and left just as the opening bars of Beethoven's Pastoral Symphony, issuing from an unnoticed wireless set, pierced the room's squalor like a sword.

I spent some time alone by the sea, no smell of sewage there and less likelihood of contracting prickly heat, a maddening skin ailment flourishing in the city. Against a beach blindingly white the Atlantic rollers roared and crashed and on sandhills casuarina trees sighed, whispered and sang like Aeolian harps, the beach itself swarming with little prickly crabs which scuttled from under foot with derisive gestures and nipped sharply when captured. I swam, dozed under the trees or gazed seaward, wondering what effect continuing war might have produced on the hearts of friends at home. I could hardly look for a hero's welcome, and to the inevitable question 'What have you been doing?' no answer in the least dramatic came to mind.

At length, no ship appearing, those of us who had waited longest were flown to Freetown, where there was said to be a better chance of one. The Hudson followed the indentations of the Guinea coast, flying at about 8,000 feet, below us the Atlantic Ocean, painted green and turquoise blue, wrinkled breakers showing as white thread, while inland for thousands of square miles forest clothed the earth like fur.

If it be true that events the most keenly anticipated are those most certain to disappoint, my leave proved the exception. The ship in which I travelled home turned out to be a well-appointed liner, on board as passengers numbers of white women and children evacuated from Ceylon, threatened at the time, or said to be, by the implacable Japanese. By chance rather than design I found myself engaged in a transient love affair. All officers going home on leave had to form crews for manning day and night the Oerlikon anti-aircraft guns on the upper deck, and both of us found it disconcerting that one of my crew should choose to knock on the door of the lady's cabin at four in the morning to announce that it was nearly time for me to report for duty. We had prided ourselves on circumspection.

In England, despite my doubts, on the surface nothing much seemed altered. It was joy to shed uniform, to fish in a clear stream meandering through water-meadows, stay at Brown's Hotel in Dover Street, dine and dance at the Berkeley. I went so far as to make love with somebody's adjutant, a situation not before envisaged. She was a captain in the ATS.

Jack Symons, whom I had arranged to meet in England and introduce to my family, returned to Nigeria on the same boat as myself, but not to the 10th Battalion. Reclaimed by the colonial service, he became private secretary to the Chief Commissioner in the big red-roofed house at Kaduna. Though for Jack it was an infinitely more congenial job I was to miss him badly.

# CHAPTER 7

# Orders for Burma

During my absence on leave the 10th Battalion had changed station from Kaduna to Sokoto, an old city in the semi-desert country of the extreme north-west. The Sultan of Sokoto, the only sultan in Nigeria, was spiritual leader of all Muslims in the Western Sudan and a potentate of great dignity and presence. (He descended from Osman Dan Fodio, the Fulani conqueror who, a hundred years before, had with sword and spear carried Islam's green banner across Northern Nigeria, defeating and returning to Allah the indigenous Hausa-speaking peoples.)

Struggling to fit myself into the groove again, I felt like an opium smoker who, awakening from beguiling dreams, finds himself still in the old den beset by faces grown too familiar. There seemed nothing to look forward to now.

Within a month of my reluctant return the colonel, our third in two years, decided to organise a full scale field-firing exercise – that is, one using live ammunition – perhaps to stir up what was becoming an increasingly stagnant pond. In the course of this simulated battle I came, quite fortuituously, under fire for the first time. Already a private soldier advancing with his section just ahead of my Company Headquarters had been shot through a lung at point blank range by the careless and trigger-happy fool of a Bren gunner at his side. Seeing him fall, I had felt certain that the victim must have been acting a part, collapsing to put on a show of verisimilitude for the benefit of the British Resident and his wife, until horrified to observe that his chest bubbled with pink and frothy blood. It was no act. (Removed from the scene by stretcher bearers, the wounded man rejoined me within a couple of months.) This seemed bad enough, but as we began to climb a stony hill on the way to our objective a rifle platoon, mistaking the soldiers I was with for its cardboard figure targets, showered us liberally with bullets. They cracked overhead and between our flattened bodies, splashing and slanting from black rocks. By a miracle no man was hit, though several seconds must have elapsed before the offenders, hearing my wild and angry shouts, thought fit to divert their aim.

The author 1940.

(*Left*) Deddi Mazari, he had borrowed the corporal's stripes, to which he had no entitlement, in honour of the occasion.

(*Below*) A platoon on the march in northern Nigeria 1941. Note the 'long shorts' (which the two British leaders scorn to wear). At the rear ammunition boxes and what appears to be a Boyes anti-tank rifle are being head-toted by specially enlisted men called 'carriers', who by 1942 had disappeared from the infantry establishment.

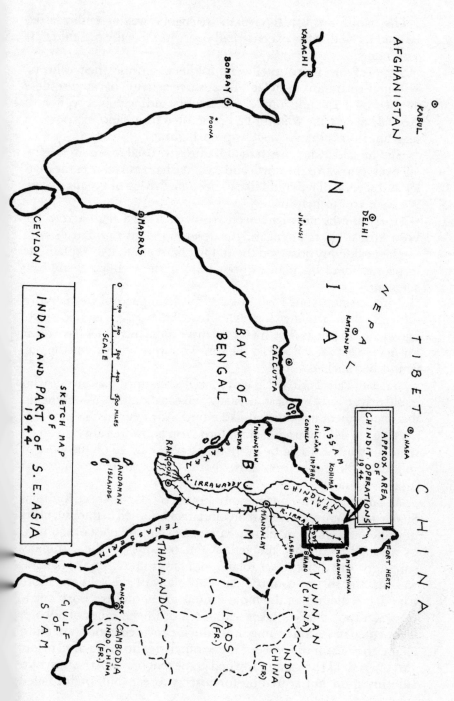

SKETCH MAP
OF
INDIA AND PART OF S.E. ASIA
1944

AFGHANISTAN

KABUL

KARACHI

BOMBAY

POONA

CEYLON

MADRAS

INDIA

JHANSI

DELHI

NEPAL

KATHANDU

TIBET

LHASA

CHINA

SCALE
0  100  200  300  400  500 MILES

BAY OF BENGAL

CALCUTTA

ASSAM

SILCHAR
IMPHAL
COMILLA

KOHIMA

APPROX AREA
OF
CHINDIT OPERATIONS
1944

ANDAMAN ISLANDS

RANGOON

TAUNGDAW

AKYAB

ARAKAN

B U R M A

R. IRRAWADDY

CHINDWIN RIVER

R. IRRAWADDY

MANDALAY

LASHIO

MOGAUNG

MYITKYINA

FORT HERTZ

YUNNAN (CHINA)

TENASSERIM

THAILAND

BANGKOK

GULF OF SIAM

LAOS (FR.)

CAMBODIA (INDO CHINA FR.)

INDO CHINA (FR.)

The handful of British civilian spectators, waxing enthusiastic, assured us all that the exercise had been 'just like the real thing'. It had indeed.

Some of my more intelligent soldiers, sensing their officers' growing frustration in default of positive activity, became restless on their own account. Yaro Zuru, an outstanding young regular of the Dakkakeri tribe whom I had promoted from lance-corporal to sergeant in less than a year, approached me.

'Sir,' he said, 'when we were in Kaduna we used to see aircraft flying over us towards the north and east. We have talked over the matter and several of us would like to become drivers of sky-machines. We wish you to help us.'

Hurricane fighters had been regularly ferried high across the West African sky to Egypt and the desert war, and Yaro Zuru's keen eye had evidently observed them. I felt hard put to it to explain the impossibility of his plan without hurting the feelings of my best sergeant.

'I understand your wish,' I said 'but flying aeroplanes is more difficult than driving lorries. Great knowledge is necessary, knowledge of books. The men who drive these machines have been for many years at school. By the time you were ready to fly the war would be finished.'

Sergeant Yaro Zuru had in his innocence assumed that anyone who could drive a lorry might straightaway take to the air, simply exchanging one element for another, like a bird. At my words his face fell.

'That we did not understand, lord. You know we cannot read or write. In truth it would be more fitting if we carried on the work of soldiers, which we know how to do.' Yaro smiled to hide his disappointment.

At Sokoto it was considerably hotter by day than at Kaduna. Shade trees were scarce and roads and tracks clothed in thick blankets of white sand which made marching an exhausting test of stamina, occasionally stopping altogether the mouths of the company songsters. But this arid scrubland, not far distant from the Sahara, was just the sort of country native to many of the soldiers, more friendly to them than the monotonous green orchard bush encircling Kaduna. Shallow lakes within ten or fifteen miles of Sokoto, frequented in season by migratory duck, provided good sport and a change of diet for the officers' mess; otherwise no distraction of any sort offered. I kept a tame crowned crane that paraded the dust outside my mud hut searching for insects to eat, but Deddi failed to appreciate the merits of the bird; he had to spend half an hour a day catching its ration of live grasshoppers.

In November we heard strong rumours that a West African formation was destined for active service overseas. Though the rumours persisted, we refused to believe there could be fire behind the smoke. Convinced that if the war lasted ten years we should never see a battlefield, and quick to discount hints that we might after all be wrong, our reiterated demands for action had begun to lack conviction; they sounded as automatic as the chanting of Orwell's sheep. I noticed that those who had clamoured loudest turned out to be the first to protest our unreadiness or unsuitability when, at the beginning of December, it became known beyond argument that at least one West African division would sail for the East to fight the Japanese in Burma. Our immediate reaction to news so momentous might be compared to that of ship-wrecked mariners who, continually hoping to see a sail, find themselves so frequently disappointed that they accept their eventual deliverance without much emotion, as though stunned. In any case we hadn't yet been told which of the many West African battalions would be selected. Nine would be needed to form an infantry division, of these no more than three or four likely to be from Nigeria.

Redoubling training tempo I drove the B Company men hard; but after Christmas 1942 – my third in Nigeria – learnt that whether or not I should see active service it wouldn't be with them. I was promoted temporary major and posted to the 7th Battalion at Kano, a cruel blow which a month earlier I might better have sustained. To be forced to abandon B Company immediately a chance of taking it into action arose seemed ironical indeed. Having raised it from within a few months of its birth, watched over it through childhood and adolescence to maturity, I knew every company name and face – had known all but a score for two years – and to wear a crown instead of three stars meant nothing compared to the loss of my command.

Before bidding the traditional formal farewell to the whole of B Company on parade, at Duggy Pott's suggestion I invited every African non-commissioned officer, from new lance-corporal to the excellent Dakkakeri Sergeant-Major Isa Rambo (who had succeeded Labo) to a party. Congo beer as well as gallons of palm wine were provided; Deddi and others made savouries and sweetmeats which with hundreds of cigarettes he arranged on mats laid on the brown turf outside my hut. My guests were at first subdued. Conscious of the occasion, unsure of what might be expected of them, the African NCOs thought it safest to assume long faces and a lugubrious demeanour, like mourners attending a Church of England funeral. Mercifully they rapidly became more at ease, swilling beer of both sorts and making the usual ribald jokes, slapping each other on the back and heartily belching. Sergeant Yaro Zuru, not only a fine soldier but a mimic of uncanny skill, first put away great quantities of drink and then scrambled swaying to his feet and treated us to a series of satirical imitations of B Company's white officers and sergeants. Attitudes, gestures, voices – every absurd idiosyncrasy was guyed by Yaro to deadly effect, every outward facet of character mercilessly exposed. All of us rocked with laughter; sweat streamed down faces black and white. Had my left hand always twitched in that ridiculous manner whenever I drilled the company? And did my parade ground voice really sound so strangled?

Some hours elapsed before all jugs were empty and the party over. Sergeant Major Isa Rambo, less of a talker than old Labo Kontagora, delivered a brief, incoherent speech of thanks before marching his NCOs back to their lines in the best order they could muster. One of them started up the verse of a marching song and every man swelled the loud chorus. Standing amid the debris of the feast, close to tears, I listened to the powerful voices rising, falling and then fading in the distance.

A few days after that I travelled in a fifteen hundredweight truck from Sokoto to Kano with Deddi, the pet crane and what little baggage I possessed.

The 7th Battalion happened to be one of three from Nigeria forming part of the first West African Division bound for the East; and I was left in no doubt that the presence of a new major in the Kano officers' mess excited among its members something more than the usual distrust. The company commanders, very stiff, must have wondered why I should have been promoted before one of themselves; indeed I understand that the Commanding Officer, Colonel Gillmore, had had every intention of filling the major's vacancy with an officer of his own choice. It was a bad beginning. Not since joining my own regiment at Colchester in 1936 had I felt so little wanted. B Company of the 10th my whole military world, so long as company affairs flourished satisfactorily I had concerned myself little with the rest of the battalion, never in any case a unit closely-knit. The 7th possessed a spirit and cohesion I had found absent at Kaduna and Sokoto and partly for that reason too its officers resented me as an interloper.

Nonetheless the company I now took over struck me as poorly trained. Before I had time even to discover the names of my principal subordinates we were sent out on exercises in the sandy scrub, our 'enemy' the Divisional Reconnaissance Regiment, half British and half African in composition and armed with light tanks. As soon as they caught sight of tanks rumbling towards their weapon pits, as one man my new soldiers leapt out of them and fled incontinent to the rear! However amusing or ludicrous this shameful scuttle might look in retrospect, at the time I was appalled, indeed shocked to the core, and gave the NCOs a tremendous and prolonged telling off. That they had never before set eyes on tanks 'attacking' them could be no excuse for conduct so cowardly: B Company would have stood its ground, I felt certain. How on earth would these Africans react when faced with Japanese, in tanks or out of them?

The news of their impending departure to India en route for the Burma front had been received phlegmatically enough by the soldiers of the 7th Battalion. It was as Allah willed; their knowledge of the world, their imagination too limited to allow them to picture for themselves scenes so distant. Burma, the South Seas or the North Pole: it mattered not. Wherever their white officers should choose to lead them they were pledged to follow; had they not promised to do so when they signed up? Ordered to travel skyward in a rocket and invade some hostile planet, the Nigerians might – probably would – have expressed no surprise. Throughout February men were sent off in great batches to their villages for embarkation leave, the British working at their desks meanwhile, sleeping away the afternoon heat and in the evenings visiting the Kano club to play snooker, drink or flirt with the few nursing sisters available.

The colonel (who was nearing the end of a long 'tour') departed for leave in England; his second-in-command, pronounced physically unfit, was 'invalided' and as the next senior officer I handed over my new company and placed myself in temporary command. Much demanded to be done, the battalion about to leave Kano for Ibadan, far to the south, to train for jungle warfare in the depths of the rain forest spread in a dense mat over southern Nigeria. Detailed planning thus became necessary, but I had been left a con-

scientious and intelligent adjutant and with the quartermaster's
more professional help most of the administrative problems sorted
themselves out. In April of 1943, when the last man had returned
from his village – what can he have said to family and friends, I wondered, and they to him? – the 7th Battalion marched singing down
the road to Kano station and there subaltern and sergeant strove to
fit black flocks into carriage compartments that seemed incapable of accommodating the press of heavily accoutred and sweating soldiers. Bustle, cursing and calling out of names continued
until finally, when every man had been squeezed into place, the
engine groaned and the long line of coaches shuffled away from
Kano to the south. Glistening faces peered from every carriage window, cheering and laughing; buglers in resurrected crimson cum-
merbunds sounded stirring farewell fanfares from the platform.

Quartered in school buildings three or four miles from Ibadan,
we were happy to find ourselves surrounded by gardens of flowering trees and creepers set amid green lawns, very pleasing to the eye
after Kano's scrub and dust. In this lush Southern world everything
was brightly coloured, dreamlike, the sombre greys and duns of
Northern Nigeria another continent. The city of Ibadan itself
sprawled over a big area in a confusion of ugly, rusting galvanised
iron roofs, houses and mean streets providing homes for as many
goats and draggle-feathered poultry as Africans. The goats, black
and white, possessed legs too short for their bodies; it was as if some
inches had been sawn off them by Pan's carpenter for reasons
unknown. As a result the animals walked jerkily, marionettes on strings,
at night, indifferent to traffic, sleeping in the streets like down-and-
outs.

From the comparative isolation of the commanding officer's
chair I had to busy myself with jungle training areas, firing ranges,
the drafting of training memoranda and a thousand and one other
matters. Even a provisional headmaster must remain a little apart;
but at least by this time I had become accepted even by the more
entrenched staff. The initial period of coolness was forgotten.

Colonel Gillmore, whose many merits all appreciated, returned
from leave after his battalion had been in the south for perhaps a
month. He appointed me to command Z Company, and not before
time I had opportunity to assess the officers and men with whom I
expected one day to confront the Japanese. Promising enough
material, the Z Company Africans needed, I considered, intensive
training if they were to realise their potential and with the help of

my officers I did my best. As well as putting them through number-less 'dry' jungle exercises, we loosed off hundreds of light machine gun and rifle rounds just over the soldiers' backs as they crawled forward, exploding booby traps and other devices in all directions with profligate and probably dangerous abandon: this 'battle inoculation', so-called, designed to accustom men of limited imagination to the noise of shells bursting and bullets cracking close overhead. The bright, parabolic streaks carved through the air by our tracers were as fascinating to watch as fireworks.

The primary equatorial jungle in which we often trained evoked wonder and awe rather than simple aesthetic pleasure. Here mon-strous evergreen trees, locked in a life-and-death struggle one with another, reared straight upward to burst into leaf far overhead, knotted vines thicker than ropes writhing about their trunks like the serpents round the body of Laocoon. Dank smells of burgeoning and decaying vegetable matter pervaded all. One had the impres-sion that the forest visibly expanded, tendrils uncurling, buds opening and trees pressing upward before one's very eyes, like those speeded-up botanical nature films which used once to be shown in cinemas before the main picture.

From some wandering fellow I was foolish enough to buy a hen ostrich. It wasn't a pet to inspire devotion and spared none for its patron. Treacherous, expensive to keep, my ostrich consumed grain in vast quantities, and though it may have reminded Deddi of his childhood on the Sahara's edge, his dislike of the Sokoto crowned crane was nothing compared to the hatred this bird aroused in him. Long eye-lashes and beautiful dusky liquid eye belied its true nature; any man, white or black, approaching too close to the beast as it strutted about on the lawns would immediately be put to flight, its one creditable act in my eyes having been to chase the new battalion second-in-command, a plump man, up a tree, or so it was reported. A fortnight after I had acquired it the ostrich sustained an enor-mous gash along one flank, obviously inflicted by an African soldier's matchet; and though Neil Leitch, the battalion doctor, after anaesthetising the creature skilfully sewed up the long wound with lengths of string, a few days later the ostrich disappeared in mysterious circumstances. I had my suspicions about the motive for its abduction and could guess where the carcase might have ended up.

The date of embarkation for India drew ever closer. When the final inspection had been held, the last packing-case lid screwed down, the last pair of correctly-sized new boots issued, the Sultan of Sokoto himself came down from the north to wish our men good fortune. The battalion paraded in a 'hollow square', and as he walked slowly down the stiff ranks the soldiers, awed, followed every movement of the princely white-robed figure from the corners of their eyes. The Sultan paused to say a word to every Nigerian sergeant and sergeant-major, placing his long and shapely hands on each of their shaven heads and murmuring a blessing. Then he addressed the whole battalion. 'May Allah keep you safe, may Allah grant that you return victorious, my children.'

Two days after the Sultan's visit we sailed. There was no brass band or other farewell pageantry, neither cheering nor handkerchief's sad flutter; we embarked unnoticed, almost furtively, and as the troop-ship gathered way the low Guinea coast began imperceptibly to melt into the afternoon haze.

# CHAPTER 8

# To be a Chindit

To see white men who worked always with their hands, wore dirty clothes, assumed no authority and were inclined to slap them on the back was a revelation to the African troops, and possibly they surprised the ship's crew equally. At their officers' meal-times black soldiers might be seen slyly peeping through the saloon windows, gratified to observe that we were waited upon by stewards with skins as pale as our own. It enhanced our prestige, theirs too. (Whites such as these sailors and, later, the ordinary soldiers of British regiments, classifiable neither as officers nor 'colour sergies', administrators or traders, were to remain a puzzle to our men.) Though none of the Northerners, nor many Southerners, had seen the sea before, marine marvels like schools of porpoises and flying fish were quickly taken for granted. The Nigerian in the ranks seldom sought to unravel seams unfamiliar, like many an educated man relying on others to produce explanations while reserving the right to doubt them. The white seamen got on excellently with the black soldiers, laughing and smoking with them and exchanging small possessions: heart-warming indeed to watch the two races doing their best to communicate, without the least touch of distrust or prejudice.

Dredged-up English lessons served to kill time, but I found it more profitable, or anyway more interesting, to talk to the troops about the war, the Japanese and the world.

'You understand? These small men are the King of England's enemies, and so yours too. If they are not defeated they will enslave many – perhaps even yourselves!'

'What! Enslave us black men? Certainly not!' the soldiers would exclaim. 'We would never allow it, no indeed, and soon with Allah's help we shall destroy hundreds of small yellow ones, just as our brothers killed Italians. No doubt some of us will be killed also, if it be Allah's will. All men must die and only He knows at what hour their day will end!'

This unclouded confidence disturbed me. The Nigerians simply couldn't believe that Japanese would turn out to be a completely different kettle of fish from Italians. Our men had inherited the bombast of an earlier age, when before battle was joined each side would loudly proclaim its own martial virtues and pour shouted scorn upon the supposed shortcomings of the enemy.

When eventually we reached the South African coast, the Durban authorities were pleased to permit our men on shore for official route marches to stretch their legs provided they carried no weapons; it would never have done for a native of Natal to see black men armed with rifles. The Durban attitude was at least less rigid than that of Capetown, where shore visits by our Africans had been banned altogether. Black troops, with arms or without, could on no account be acknowledged to exist.

White officers and non-commissioned ranks had the time of their lives in Durban. The young ladies of Natal, a high proportion of whom claimed British descent, couldn't do enough for those they quaintly termed 'Imperials', ignoring their own stalwart-looking and bronzed men (who shocked us by wearing shorts as brief as miniskirts) in favour of the most insignificant-looking British officer or sergeant, just as English and Scottish girls at home had gone overboard for Americans and Poles. The citizens of Durban had, I believe, entertained several boatloads of troops already and one could reasonably suppose they would have grown blasé, but not a bit of it. Hospitality was limitless; one might be picked up in hotel, in the street, almost anywhere by some charming girl anxious to assist in every way within her scope. That we commanded black troops and had smelt no whiff of gunpowder failed to prevent us from being fêted as heroes, spoilt almost to death for ten days of eating, drinking and lovemaking. In retrospect Durban appears as a golden city, a southern paradise, the stuff of sensuous dreams; and I for one have never forgotten its delights.

Well guarded by warships, our convoy reached India without external misadventure but a number of soldiers succumbed to pneumonia, a disease uncommon or unknown in Nigeria. The sufferers became frightened, abandoned hope, closed their eyes and quietly died.

The Bombay sky was like tarnished brass, the morning air as empty of vitality as an old man's breath. Seven years had gone by since as an over-anxious, unhappy and very junior subaltern I had disembarked at Bombay en route to join the 1st Battalion of my regiment in Poona.

From the very first the West African troops disdained all Indians, men lighter in the hue than they and with features more delicate, indiscriminately dubbing them 'Indus' and perceiving at once that they must be members of a subject race. From the superior height of the deck our soldiers would glare in mock ferocity at the coolies lounging on the wharf, criticising their solemn manners and skinny bodies and exclaiming in horror whenever an Indian squirted into the dust his blood-red jet of betel-juice. Had these 'Indus' some fatal disease?

At Bombay we heard important news. The Nigerian Brigade was to be severed from the 81st West African Division and form part of the Long Range Penetration Force, the Chindits, organised and trained to fight behind the Japanese front in Northern Burma, its begetter and commander General Orde Wingate. Though flattered to serve under a soldier whose remarkable exploits and unconventional character the newspapers and wireless bulletins had already made much of, our hearts a little misgave us. Since nearly every officer and nine tenths of the men were untested in any kind of warfare, the task ahead of us would certainly prove daunting.

The battalion made its first camp near a village called Talbahat, about thirty miles from Jhansi, in country that didn't strike us as ideal for progressive jungle training. Scarcely a tree stood within sight; here were only boulders, isolated bushes, dust, scorpions and withered grass, reminding the Africans of Kano or Sokoto.

Close to our camp, on a brown knoll overlooking a lake, stood an ancient temple and a broken fort, ruins reflected stone by stone in calm grey water. The temple steps, worn down by generations of devoted feet, continued down into the lake itself, which must long ago have been a great deal shallower. It was a beautiful and deserted spot, and if the dogs of war may once have hunted here they surely would no longer. The lakeside became my sanctuary. Wandering there when time could be spared, I would indulge myself in absurd – and in such peaceful surroundings wholly inappropriate – dreams of glory. I led forlorn assaults, stood blood-soaked but triumphant, surrounded by tidy enemy corpses, received thanks and decorations for my services.

To fit our new rôle the battalion required to be reorganised drastically, split, amoeba-like, into two equal parts or 'columns', each designed for independent action. Column rather than battalion was the basic unit of Wingate's force, its nucleus a swollen, extra powerful rifle company. This meant the sacrifice of two of our existing four.

For three days we were kept on tenterhooks while colonel and

battalion second-in-command decided fates. For me, of course, the
vital issue was whether Z Company would draw the long straw or
the short, live or die. With my own second-in-command to give
moral support I sat up until late at night trying to read Colonel
Gillmore's mind, composing in advance plausible grounds for protest should his decision go against Z Company. I could have
shouted with relief when told of our survival, indeed augmentation.
The column of which an enlarged Z Company now formed the
fighting basis was designated 'Number 29' and commanded by the
Colonel; the other, built round X Company under Nobby Hall, a
lowland Scot jealous for his men's good name, numbered 35 and
headed by the battalion second-in-command. No 29 Column's
staff officer, Chris Harrison, a first-rate, most likable man from the
Colonial Service, fully deserved the special confidence our commanding officer placed in his ability; he it was, indeed, whose promotion from captain had been deferred by my unpopular posting
to Kano ten months before.

At the beginning of December 1943 our emergent columns, now
much to our gratification clad in jungle-green trousers instead of
those hated long shorts, played the part of 'enemy' to a Chindit
brigade whose training had been nearly completed and whose
attainments were to be assessed by General Wingate himself. Having camouflaged our defensive position so effectively that it
remained undiscovered, we seldom caught sight of opponents.
Occasionally, however, when the bowed figures of 'enemy' soldiers
tramped within range we made brave sallies from our secret
stronghold to return in triumph with a few prisoners. Crowding
round our British and Gurkha captives, the Africans stared at them
as though at strange beasts, making the most of this first close view
of their Chindit allies. If British private soldiers should prove a
novelty, it was Gurkhas who aroused interest more intense.

'But this kind of Indu is very strong!' the Nigerians remarked.
'They do not at all resemble those we have already seen. Small – yet
look at the great loads they carry on their backs! And such curious
faces, like pictures of Japans!'

Whether British or Gurkha, the prisoners struck us as hardy,
determined and tough. The Africans, noting this, looked thought-
ful, their obstinate complacency perhaps not entirely impregnable.
If men like these had, up to now, failed to defeat the Japanese, what
must 'Japans' themselves be like?

Although we hadn't yet seen him in person Wingate's name was constantly on our lips, his prestige enormous, his influence all-pervasive. The name 'Wingate' conjured up a figure renowned but remote, a being beyond praise or derision, a personality dominating our military thought and action as thoroughly as though we saw him daily. Before we had abandoned our exercise stronghold he arrived out of the blue. It was evening, the day's work over; dirty and dishevelled as we found ourselves, the peremptory summons for officers to assemble left no time for tidying up. Reaching the rendezvous breathless and last I saw a small, rather insignificant-looking man walking towards us. The stranger, bare-headed, as scruffy as ourselves, seemed ill-at-ease. When he came closer and I noticed the red tabs and DSO ribbon with two bars on the crumpled tunic I felt disappointed. Could this stooping, unmilitary-looking figure really be Wingate himself? I overheard the Colonel ask our visitor if he wished for introduction to the officers by name, but the General shook his head, mumbling something I failed to catch, eyes fixed on the ground.

Then, alert and looking straight at us, Wingate began to talk rapidly and passionately, words tumbling. His mind teemed with ideas and images, his thoughts seemed to leap ahead of harshly delivered words. The power, the certainty radiating from this wolfish-looking man held us in thrall. When he had finished speaking there wasn't an officer among us having the least doubt of what Wingate required of him – of all of us – in Burma. We knew exactly how the Japanese would react to Wingate's plans and how our commander would impose his will upon them. When he had finished speaking none had a question to ask; none but would follow wherever he might lead.

For second-in-command Z Company I had Dicky Lambert, a fiercely enthusiastic, forthright and loyal man and constant support. In his thirties, vigorous and strongly built, devoted alike to beer and company, Dicky had a rocky face, a wide mouth and close-set eyes which protruded slightly, like buttons. He relished a tilt at the regular army hierarchy, its staff officers in particular, and the more beer he had put away the more emphatic Dicky became, often collecting round himself an ironically applauding audience – a Hyde Park orator in uniform. He came from Newcastle and had been a government auditor in pre-war Nigeria. Three of my four platoon commanders had also served with Z Company ever since I had taken it over at Ibadan and I find it impossible to draw dispassionate sketches of men I came to know so well; they, and Dicky also, remain too close to get into focus. Denis Arnold, about twenty-four or five, tall and good-looking with regular features and great charm, his laugh ringing, had his bêtes noires but was more likely than not to believe good of his fellow men. In Burma, Denis' deceptive vagueness cast aside, he revealed himself in true colours as an able and courageous platoon commander. Tich Cooper, once a pre-war regular soldier in the ranks and recently commissioned, was a dashing, cocky, self-assertive, tough little man who, having been at the receiving end of things, knew every detail of his job and comfortably withstood our attempts at leg-pulling. Younger than Denis, Steve Elvery was the only officer besides myself to have been to a public school, whatever that might have been worth. Ebullient, he gave the impression of being scatterbrained, but Steve, resembling a small and raffish bird, proved as capable as excitable, war maturing but failing to sober him. My youngest officer, a big, clumsy bear called 'Blossom' Eede became commander of my added fourth platoon after the battalion had been re-organised. A bright red bloom suffused Eede's downy cheeks; hence the soubriquet of Blossom.

The British company sergeant-major, Kitt, was a quiet soft-spoken Cornishman who enjoyed the company of the African NCOs and would talk to his black subordinates by the hour in most uncertain Hausa. One of several peculiarities of his was to make military predictions of the gloomiest nature imaginable. Evidently they afforded Kitt considerable satisfaction, and if one should turn out to be less than accurate there would always be another ready to take its place. Far from being a barrack square type of soldier, nor indeed everybody's idea of a sergeant-major, Kitt was a conscientious and loyal man and Z Company his life: I wouldn't have exchanged him for warrant officer more conventional. Sergeants Speak and Tanner, the one tall and fair-haired, the other small and dark, completed the company roll of British.

In Umoru Numan, Denis Arnold's platoon sergeant, and Adamu Hadeijia, Steve's right hand man, Z Company possessed two exceptionally able African non-commissioned officers. Umoru – unusually – was a literate Christian of Pagan Adamawa stock, Adamu Hadeijia a Muslim, black and square-faced, a serious-minded, religious man. How I wished I had been able to take with me to the 7th Battalion the Pagan Dakkakeri Sergeant Yaro Zuru from B Company, my particular protégé, to make the third of a distinguished black triumvirate all of different faiths!

The young men briefly, reluctantly and most inadequately described were those with whom, as their company commander, I found myself closely associated throughout most of the working day or night, now and for months to come. If none would have regarded himself as in any respect out of the common, or dream of posing as a pattern for military perfection, Roman centurion having subordinates half so capable and enthusiastic, loyal and steadfast in adversity would have thought himself blessed by his tutelary god. It is novelist or script-writer who seems invariably to portray soldiers thrown together at random as hateful to one another.

As the weeks passed so the two 7th Battalion columns tended to drift a little away from each other, as self-contained units must, each acquiring its own particular character. But our ties were always to remain strong. We were blood brothers, indeed twins, rivalry between us never serious. In Nigeria I had become too self- sufficient to interest myself in those outside a narrow circle, but now, intimacy more or less forced upon us, changed into a partisan as keen as any, No 29 Column the fountain-head of my allegiance. We felt proud to be Chindits, the prospect of fighting the Japanese behind the front (however tenuously a front existed) having a romantic appeal to be sensed by the least imaginative. Scoff we might, but without going so far as to talk about it we felt ourselves dedicated to a mission of high endeavour. Our cynicism was skin-deep, a mask.

In the jungles of the Central Provinces we turned into a nomad tribe. After exhausting the training possibilities of one patch of jungle both columns would pack up, march some miles and pitch camp in another, sleeping in crude huts flung together by the soldiers from branches, leaves and grass. When stars had rushed into the sky and the night air cooled the rocks, officers of No 29 Column would sit round big log fires and talk, from time to time waving aromatic wood smoke from their eyes. The faces of my companions, half in shadow, would look soft and relaxed, suddenly innocent, the faces of boys. Close contact cemented us; the shy seemed to become less diffident, the talkative readier to listen, the selfish more considerate; and since trivial matters were apt to assume an unwarranted importance and be long debated, often we sat until past midnight. Then someone would kick the fire's dying embers, releasing streams of red and orange sparks, upon which ritual act we would grope our way into the night, each to his hut.

Colonel Gillmore, promoted to command the Nigerian Brigade, said goodbye to his 7th Battalion. There came to us from the 6th a new No 29 Column commander and battalion second-in-command called Peter Vaughan, a tall, angular Welsh Guardsman in his early thirties, talkative and good-hearted, dashing and confident. Vaughan and I chanced to have been sent on what was billed as a jungle training course, near Ibadan, both of us openly and loudly critical of every aspect of the prescribed doctrine and therefore anathema to the instructors. We had worked together as a pair, becoming very friendly.

The new colonel, he who had joined the battalion at Ibadan as second-in-command and – possibly – been chased up a tree by my ostrich, remained in charge of No 35 Column and of course supervised the work of No 29 as well.

At about this period I was granted a few days' local leave and travelled by train to Delhi with my 'boy' Deddi, who was anxious to see something of an Indian city. I took him in a taxi all round New Delhi and Old, and as we passed the Red Fort Deddi enquired who had built it. 'Indus', I told him. Tears came into his eyes. No Africans could produce anything like it in a thousand years, he murmured sadly. It was the reaction of an unusually sensitive man. (When after our campaign I took a party of Nigerian soldiers to look at the Taj Mahal, no such emotion was shown. After gazing politely at the great mausoleum for a moment or two their attention was caught by a performing bear led by some ragged entertainer. At once they gathered round it, exclaiming in wonder and astonishment. The Taj Mahal might not have existed.)

At Delhi I fell seriously ill and was compelled to spend a fortnight in a military hospital, needing another week in which to recuperate before being considered strong enough to rejoin No 29 Column. Our recently appointed colonel, so I heard, had done his best to dump me on the grounds that I couldn't recover the required peak of fitness in time for operations but been dissuaded by Peter Vaughan, for which I blessed him.

In Burma, Chindit columns were to be maintained entirely by air, supplies of every kind dropped to us by parachute. Mules would carry loads too heavy for men – loads such as wireless sets and their batteries, machine guns and mortars with their ammunition, 'bullion', medical supplies and so forth – and a number of column ponies be provided for wounded and sick to sit on until evacuation

Z Company officers at Ibadan 1943. From left to right: Lt Arnold, Capt Lambert, the author, Lt Cooper, Lt Elvery. This is the photograph I recalled so vividly in Burma (see page 108).

Z Company: C.S.M. Kitt is in the centre, myself on his left. Lambert is behind on his right, and Arnold behind to his left. The two Nigerians—unusually small—are Z Coy office orderly and storeman. Elvery is on the left of the photograph and Sergeant Tanner on the right.

The author on leave from Nigeria in 1942.

by air became possible. Everything else had to be carried by the soldier himself, his enormous pack, bulging with extra pouches sewn on, the trademark of a Chindit, be he brigadier or private. In packs, in haversacks, in front pouches or slung from a shoulder there would be food for a maximum of five days, a blanket, a change of underclothing and perhaps a pair of shorts, spare socks, canvas shoes, a canvas water container called a chagul, washing gear, water bottle, personal weapon and many rounds of ammunition, plus – for officers – field-glasses and compass. After a 'supply drop' a pack would turn the scales at about seventy pounds. No kind of baggage animal, not even a mule, is able to carry so high a proportion of its own weight as a man. Scarcely able to stir a step under loads so intolerable, at first we found training marches agony, sweat streaming from our faces, backs and spirits alike near to breaking, legs buckling under us. But with practice pack-toting capacity began to improve, and in a month we had developed into satisfactory beasts of burden. Unless of herculean physique, however, no soldier could run more than a few paces with full pack, the best he could do to shamble along like a bear. The only sort of compensation was that once a Chindit had dumped his load after the day's march he felt light as a feather and fancied he could leap two dozen feet into the sky. An exhilarating physical sensation – one thought of it as like walking on the moon – it would invariably be accompanied by a corresponding rise in spirits.

Supply drops, whether by day or night, made a brave show. Preparations for them were elaborate. After firewood had been collected a number of separate bonfires in the shape of a long L would be laid ready for lighting, parties of soldiers take up position ready to defend the 'dropping zone' (carefully selected so as not to endanger low-flying aircraft), mules brought up close ready to carry away loads so that they could be broken down under cover, men told off to disentangle the parachutes and pick up containers. Finally at the appointed moment the fires would be lit, smoke-wreaths rise and with luck the Dakotas drone overhead. When the parachutes, looking like huge toadstools, fell drunkenly from the aircrafts' bellies the Africans would gaze upwards in delight, exclaiming as they watched the containers swinging ponderously from side to side until with satisfying thumps they struck the earth. Items not susceptible to damage, such as boots or mule fodder, would be thrown out of aircraft in free bundles and hurtle to the ground at ninety miles an hour. Columns were likely enough to have a man or two killed by these, unfortunates failing to take cover in time or mis-judging where the lethal bundles would crash down.

Our mules caused a minor sensation when they at length appeared. The Nigerians, familiar with horse-flesh, had never seen such animals as mules, nor entirely believed their officers when told the beasts were to take the place of the ubiquitous three-ton lorry. Mules came in various sizes according to the weight or load they were expected to carry, the big animals mountainous, the small ones hardly bigger than donkeys, all of ours already half-trained. Every mule requiring a leader, or muleteer, to look after and load it, volunteers proved hard to find; to drive a truck or lorry regarded as civilised and splendid but to tend mule or pony a job scarcely in keeping with a fighting man's dignity. The Nigerians showed skill with the animals, all the same, and within a short while the once-reluctant muleteer, by now well warmed to his beast, was refusing to exchange his charge for Bren gun or mortar.

At this stage I lost Deddi. Our 'boys', not trained to march or fight, would have been millstones round our necks in Burma and all found themselves banished to an Indian camp to await their masters' return from operations. I missed Deddi very much. Knowing each other so well, our relationship had developed into something much more than that between master and man, his emotional pride, transitory black moods and bursts of talk and laughter a part of my life; and though nobody could adequately replace him, upon the youthful shoulders of Garaba Gonari, my soldier orderly, fell Deddi's mantle.

Garaba, hardly more than a boy, shy and with a monkey face, an engaging smile and soft slow voice, had been my orderly for some months already. If lacking Deddi's fire and personality he was a nice and willing lad and I felt responsible for him. Garaba's extreme youth was a reproach to those who had accepted his enlistment.

With Garaba Gonari as eyes, ears and compass I used to hunt at dawn through dry jungle very like that in which I had shot my tiger years before. Armed with a service rifle, constantly on the lookout for sambhur or nilghai antelope to add variety to the Africans' rations, often I wandered a fair distance without bothering in the least to consider where I might be in relation to camp. Garaba knew by instinct, and as soon as the word was given would set off in a bee-line. There could be no question of memorising landmarks; we always returned by different routes. In country totally foreign to him Garaba's exact and unfailing sense of direction, a natural gift more or less atrophied in the white man, never failed to amaze me. I shot several sambhur and guided by Garaba, who knew to within feet where they lay dead, parties would set off from camp to carry or drag the carcases to the nearest motorable track, whence they would be collected by one of our few remaining lorries and end up in the Z Company cooking pots.

To our surprise the soldiers seemed not to miss their women, their drink and other urban delights of Hausa cities. Invincibly complacent, they despised such Indian peasants as they came across and treated the camp charwallah with haughty and swaggering disdain. We British had dreaded assaults on women. But there was none, 'Indu' females unappealing to the Nigerians or else too fleet of foot.

Sergeant Umoru Numan (whom I have mentioned) organised unofficial Christian services for the rank and file and on Sunday mornings the unlikely cadences of traditional Welsh hymns sounded from Indian jungle. The singers would not all be baptised Christians: less confident of their personal Jujus now that war's breath blew warm on their cheeks, some of the animist pagans flirted with the Christian faith, thinking it wise to hedge their bets. No Muslim, or nominal Muslim, ever took part, the stern Adamu Hadeijia making sure that even the weakest in the Prophet's ranks held out against Umoru's proselytizing zeal.

Off duty the Tivs, always ready to put on a show, danced as indefatigably as in bush clearings by the Benue river; pagans sang reedy chants and twanged archaic instruments; laughter and voices raised in cheerful argument drifted through the woods, filling the Indian air with alien vitality.

Often I would walk round the various fires as the light faded.

'Greetings of the evening, Corporal Sule.'

'Greetings, master. You are well?'

'I am well, Corporal Sule. Are you missing your wife?'

'My wife? Yes indeed, truly. But I have my blanket!'

'Oh! Oh! What a thing to say!' put in another corporal, 'I have forgotten mine entirely. This is my wife now – here with me.'

He patted his rifle.

'What is the talk about?'

'We are talking, sir, about these Indu men. They keep cows, many cows though thin ones, and what do they do with them when they die? Why, one is told their carcases are left to the vultures. These Indus are fools, most certainly.'

'But Sule, cows are Jujus to these men, don't you understand? Animals whose meat they must not touch. Haven't you black men many Jujus?'

'Truly we have. But fancy not eating beef! To waste all that meat is foolish past belief. The Indu is a savage, a man of the bush. As for his women in their blue clothes, why, they run if one so much as looks at them!'

# CHAPTER 9

# Crossing the Rubicon

Towards the end of February 1944 the battalion travelled by train to Assam, crossing the immense Brahmapatra river, our Rubicon, anywhere east of which was an 'operational area'. Tich Cooper, sent on some days ahead with an advanced party, met us at the final railway station – a small, alert and bustling figure in the darkness. Our new camp, tented for a change, had been pitched by Tich's party on a hillside bristling with bamboo: by now I had lost count of the number of times we had pitched and struck. All around us were tea plantations carved out from forested slopes and on level ground lay paddi fields, dry and hard as iron at this season; Lalaghat airfield, from which we expected on some day as yet unspecified to fly into Burma, less than two miles from our tents. At Lalaghat the waiting Dakotas would roar from time to time like chained beasts, throwing clouds of dust high into the sky. Satellite gliders stood near them; we had a boozy evening of it with the American glider pilots, one of the most lively of whom turned out to be Jacky Coogan, famous as a boy actor with Charlie Chaplin in the days of silent film and full of entertaining and scandalous stories.

On the edge of the airfield Brigadier Calvert's 77 Chindit Brigade, restless in bivouac, awaited the word to fly secretly into the heart of Upper Burma by glider. At last, on the evening of 5th March, 77 Brigade's transporting aircraft, sharp against the sky, droned overhead in long and ragged procession. Awed, speechless, we stood in groups outside our tents, watching enthralled as a stream of Dakotas, towing gliders full of men and mules and weapons, crawled steadily towards the Burma frontier. We knew that in two hours the gliders would be released to land far beyond the Chindwin river in Japanese-occupied country and guessed that some would crash as they pitched down, others be forced to loose tow-ropes permaturely in the middle of nowhere or perhaps be destroyed in the air by Japanese fighter planes. The sun went down but aircraft continued to fly overhead until their silhouetted wings merged into the darkness; we could see nothing but the pinpoint reds and greens of navigation lights. Finally the moan and throb of engines died in the distance and the indifferent stars came out to stare.

Various Chindit columns, like migrating birds, continued to fly into Burma until by the end of March few remained west of the Chindwin. No date was fixed for our own flight; it was rumoured that we might have to wait until after the monsoon, which would mean a delay of six or seven months. Touchy, irritable, we alternated between high excitement and frustration, hard physical toil alone helping us to keep alight the sometimes guttering candle of column spirit. Trained troops no more than rowing eights or tuned-up athletes can maintain indefinitely a peak of readiness.

Wingate was killed. His Mitchell bomber flew into a hillside near Bishenpur during a storm as he was returning from visits to two of his brigadiers in Burma. Wingate's name so famous, his personality to such a degree awe-inspiring and magnetic, the rumours followed by the confirmation of disaster were found scarcely credible. For days no Chindit could bring himself to believe the truth, half-expecting to hear it must be a hoax, some clever ruse to deceive the enemy. The shock was profound. We couldn't know, of course, that with him died his master plan.

At this late hour our new colonel, after no more than a month or two in charge, left us for reasons unconnected with this story and because I believed him an unsuitable choice to head our kind of adventure, I wasn't sorry. Peter Vaughan, deservedly promoted in his place, now took over No 35 Column, but as Commanding Officer of the battalion was always to display fine impartiality. This left me as the senior major in No 29 but the brigadier appointed Chris Harrison to lead it. Perfectly content with Z Company, I had given no thought to commanding a column. Nevertheless to be passed over struck a severe blow to my pride; and feeling his decision to be unjust I went hot-foot to see Brigadier Gillmore. Courteously he explained that he had always regarded Chris as outstanding, besides which as column staff officer he had from the beginning been thoroughly 'in the picture'. I mustn't suppose, said the brigadier, that he considered me in any respect unsuitable; both of us, in his opinion, were perfectly capable of taking over a column. Only after much heart-searching had he chosen Chris Harrison, confident that I would support him loyally.

Since we might be in Burma in a fortnight, there remained nothing for it but to swallow disappointment and soldier on; and as Chris had always been a friend this proved easier than I had imagined. (That after the campaign I should be promoted to command the battalion and he become my second-in-command serves to illustrate the changes and chances, the quirks of military fortune; Chris Harrison, as shall be recounted, an unwilling victim of extraneous circumstance.)

The Japanese enemy began to loom twice as large as life. While laughing dutifully at the American soldier's description, quoted in some current training pamphlet, 'Nips is man-monkeys and they run around considerable', secretly we feared them. Gravely underestimated by Wavell and others when they had first attacked Malaya, an assessment to be stood on its head within weeks, the Japanese, without using many soldiers to do it, had thoroughly beaten us – had, almost literally, run rings round us. In succession we had lost to them Malaya, Singapore and Burma and as a result thousands of British and Indian troops lay rotting in jungle prison camps. We had failed to defeat the Japanese in a single major battle.

Wingate alone, in 1943, had demonstrated on any scale that British and Gurkhas, properly trained, could use the jungle to advantage. Spread far and wide by the press, the story of his exploits had gone far to counter the insidiously creeping myth of Japanese invincibility and to raise military morale throughout India and the Arakan. Not only Wingate but prominent Chindit leaders such as Calvert and Fergusson, certain Burma Rifles officers and other notable survivors of the 1943 expedition who had lectured to us felt no exaggerated respect for the Japanese as soldiers. These men set our tone, theirs was the example we aspired to emulate. As for the Nigerians, one could but surmise how they would perform in battle against an enemy who would fight to the death rather than run or surrender. Sometimes I couldn't avoid falling victim to doubt, but contrived to keep it at arm's length. Napoleon himself had said that there were no bad soldiers, only bad officers, which if cold comfort rang true.

On 3rd April, a week after my twenty-eighth birthday, No 29 Column was engaged in practising an assault against an imaginary Japanese hilltop position near an Assam railway line on a breathlessly warm morning smelling of rain, the Africans sluggish and the British irritable and bad-tempered. Nothing went right. Chris Harrison, deciding quite properly to make us carry out the whole thing again, was beginning to give new orders to his assembled officers when an African runner, panting from camp, handed him a note from Colonel Peter Vaughan. Frowning at the interruption, Chris read it quickly and we saw his expression change.

'This looks like business,' he said. 'We've to call off this bloody   .
exercise and get back to camp at once.'

The news spread like a bush fire and immediately the column transformed itself. Apathy gave way to animation, orders, loudly shouted, were eagerly obeyed, the patient waiting mules loaded in haste and within a very few minutes the whole of No 29 Column marching towards camp.

As we tramped it became hotter and hotter. Thunder rumbled close at hand; leaves and grass-stems stood unnaturally still.

One heard African laughter and excited comment but the buzz of conversation quickly died and the men continued the short march back to camp in uneasy silence. This must surely be the decisive moment, the long-awaited sign; and swayed by mass suggestion the first reaction of the soldiers had been one of infectious enthusiasm. A little later they became individuals again with minds and hearts of their own, puppets no longer; and each man, retreating into himself, felt apprehension or relief, gloom or gladness according to his temperament.

Sent on ahead of the column, I found Peter Vaughan waiting for us, with him Nobby Hall, No 35 Column company commander. The two tall men looked just as usual and I took comfort from their faces.

'There's a great flap on now,' said Peter. 'Both columns fly in tomorrow. You, Charles, are to go tonight, with Nobby and Steve Elvery. That is if the weather holds. Doesn't look a lot like it at the moment.'

He paused and I lit a cigarette, trying to control the sudden trembling of my hands. The sky had become dramatically dark and scattered raindrops smacked against our bush hats.

'We're supposed to join Calvert's brigade in White City,' Peter went on, 'and the idea is for you and Nobby to have a general look round before the rest of us fly in. Steve and Sergeant Speak and twenty men from their platoon are wanted to unload field guns from Dakotas when you get there. It's all a bit sudden. Why in hell they couldn't have let us know sooner God only knows.'

Peter Vaughan spoke as though flying into Burma were a social function for which etiquette required invitations to be issued well in advance of the event, and as we watched the sweat-drenched column tramp in I felt a surge of affection for him.

Inside my tent it was nearly dark, rain drumming loudly on the canvas. I looked for some moments at my modest possessions: carved wooden animals, a few photographs, a strip of bright raffia matting, brass Kano ashtrays and a dozen books. With Garaba's help I packed them carefully away in a black tin box. My hands felt steadier now, which was something.

Nobby, Steve and I with the rest of the party turned up at Lalaghat airfield at six o'clock that evening, festooned with all the ugly panoply of war. It was to no purpose; rain still fell, the runways had become brown seas of mud. No Dakota would take off until sunshine had dried up the surface water and we returned to our tents (which had to be repitched) feeling foolish.

By next afternoon the sun had emerged to suck up the puddles: this time there could be no reprieve. In the cool of evening I gathered my group together by a palm-thatched hut near the middle of the airfield. Smoking many cigarettes, we fiddled with our equipment and covertly observed one another. Nobby Hall looked thoroughly dour, giving nothing away, Steve Elvery's smile flashed often, Speak whistled snatches of dance music. I felt highly keyed-up and was trying not to show it. Only the Africans, standing bunched together, chattering inconsequently, munching biscuits and chocolate bars and sniffing the heady fragrance of the rain-soaked soil, appeared altogether unmoved. The brief flowering of their imagination seemed to have died.

We waited half an hour, then an American pilot strolled over, fastening up his flying jacket.

'Let's go,' he said. 'Which is it, boys? Aberdeen or White City?'

These were code names for a recently established 'stronghold' and Calvert's road and railway block respectively. Dakota airstrips had been levelled at both.

'White City,' I said, surprised that no one had thought to tell him. It was all very casual.

'OK. You can climb in now, Major. Get well forward and have the same number of your coloured men each side to balance the ship.'

The pilot smiled and shook my hand and one by one we stepped into the dark stomach of his aircraft. After dumping our great packs by the door we sat on metal seats facing one another: it was the first time any of the Africans had been inside a plane, but the Dakota might have been another three-ton lorry for all the impression it made upon them. In our noses was the warm, pear-drop smell of 'dope' and all looked remarkably neat and ship-shape. First one, then both engines roared. The aircraft shook itself and lurched forward, in seconds the runway lights fusing together and racing by in one long golden streak as after a final thump we left the ground. Beneath us we could just distinguish forest, darkening paddi-fields and, a moment later, the thin bright path of the Chindwin river.

# CHAPTER 10

# Calvert's White City

The Dakota touched down two hours before midnight, a row of little lights seen gleaming beneath us as we circled to land all that could be discerned in the blackness. As we bumped down the rough strip hewn from paddi I remembered having been told that a village called Mawlu, occupied by Japanese, lay a mile and a half to the south of the landing ground. The aircraft creaked and slithered to a stop, engines coughing then dying. It represented our last contact with the known and for a moment or two we clung to our seats as babies about to be born must cling to the womb's safety; then the pilot opened the fuselage door and we trooped out, happy to hear some English voices and the tramp of boots. No one took the least notice of us.

Steve Elvery, after searching for a while, managed to find the gunner officer who needed help to unload the dismantled pieces of his twenty-five pounders. With Sergeant Speak and the twenty soldiers he disappeared into the night, Nobby Hall and I, hardly knowing what we ought to be doing, about to follow when to our astonishment we were hailed by name in our commanding officer's unmistakable voice.

'Hallo, Charles, hallo, Nobby! I flew in just before you to have a quick look at the place. Really, I thought you were never coming! Now I've got to fly back again and see what's happening the other end. They won't let you into the block until dawn so you'd better all doss down somewhere. There's a wrecked glider down there.' He pointed vaguely north. 'See you tomorrow or the next day. Find out the form. Japs are around somewhere.' Peter had vanished before we could utter a word.

Trailed by our orderlies, Nobby and I wandered down the edge of the aircraft. It began to drizzle, wisps of low cloud drifting over the tree tops. Occasional figures, whom we presumed to be on our side, loomed out of the blackness like spirits, then dissolved. Nobody spoke to us. This was some dark and indecipherable dream-world; nothing but Nobby's material bulk beside me lent it the smallest semblance of reality. We could hear rifle and machine gun fire, grenades exploding. Might the Japanese be attacking? Where were they? We had no idea. Eventually, however, we found the damaged glider. One wing pointed to the sky, the other lay twisted on the ground; reassuring snores, surely British, sounded from inside the fuselage. Retreating our steps as best we could we got hold of Steve and his party, finally, at two o'clock in the morning, all settling ourselves for sleep beneath the glider's protective wing. Noises of skirmishing about half a mile away broke out again but by now we felt too exhausted to worry about what was happening so long as it didn't happen right on top of us. (The shots, we were given to understand next day, had most of them been fired by Chindit patrols instructed to keep the Japanese at Mawlu occupied while Dakotas landed and took off; our own aircraft, as it happened, the very last to touch down at 'White City' until that embattled 'block' was by design abandoned some weeks subsequently.)

Nobby Hall nudged me awake at sunrise, or just after. The air breathed no menace now, white streaks of mist stroked the trees, white clouds hung in a placid sky and before very long the first sun-rays began to slant across the paddi. At our backs, to the west, we could see nothing but deep jungle. Ahead of us lay the Dakota land-ing strip and beyond it, distant a quarter of a mile, the tree-clad hil-locks of the White City block rose a few hundred feet above the rail-way line and attendant road which wound from Myitkyima southward through the long valley known to Chindits as the 'railway corridor'. Figures in jungle green with slung rifles moved here and there across the landing ground and over White City floated a thin blue veil of wood-smoke. The defenders were brewing up.

By now White City had developed into a formidable all-round defensive position in preparation for the expected Japanese assaults. It was occupied, as a rule, by five or six columns while one or two more lurked in the jungle close at hand, ample machine guns and mortars providing fire-power. The more vital of the various low hills within the system of defence had been snatched from the enemy after bloody hand-to-hand fighting by men of Calvert's 77 Brigade led by the brigadier in person (Calvert's being the glider-born formation we had watched flying towards the Burma frontier exactly a month earlier). But White City was not intended as 'stronghold' or base; this hadn't been where 77 Brigade's gliders had landed or crashed on that memorable night. Brigadier Calvert with a proportion of his force had marched here in order to seize ground suitable for the construction of a 'block' on road and railway communications, his intention being to effect a strangle-hold on the supply lines of the Japanese 18th Division.

This formation opposed our Chinese allies, who under General Stilwell's direction were believed, or supposed, to be advancing down the Hukawng valley, far to the north. The block served also a second purpose: Wingate had anticipated that a powerful defensive island set up in territory the Japanese regarded as theirs would be bound to act as a magnet and encourage an affronted enemy to batter himself to death against it. The plan, as it then existed, involved both our battalion columns, together with the 12th Nigeria, forming a permanent part of the White City garrison.

Squadron Leader Robert Thompson, Calvert's air force officer, one of whose duties it was to control the landing strip, walked over to us. He had been a vital member of Wingate's 1943 expedition.

'Sorry you couldn't get inside last night.' he said. 'But it's risky in the dark. Probably you'd have been shot!'

His lined face lit up as he smiled. Bowed under the weight of packs, our little party followed him across the open paddi. He steered us through the minefield, over the road and railway, through the red-rusty hoops of Dannert concertina wire and into the White City perimeter.

At the foot of the hills, not far from the wire, we sat down and self-consciously brewed tea, trying not to betray too openly our curiosity: soldiers in peace or war, like chameleons, always adapt to the colour of their surroundings as quickly as they can, hating to appear novices. Above us on the rough slopes British soldiers of the South Staffordshire Regiment, most of them bearded, sat by their foxholes smoking. Already almost veterans, they looked it every inch, their faces alert yet a little withdrawn. Greeting our vanguard warmly, the South Staffordshires managed to avoid familar tired jokes about black faces.

I walked to Brigade Headquarters to report our arrival, delighted to find there Francis Stuart, my quiet Indian Army friend of Poona days and earlier. Though it was six years since I had watched him fly his hawks at pigeons on the brown Deccan hills Francis appeared little altered, his face young and innocent-looking, pale and smooth as a girl's. Now Calvert's brigade-major, a most important and demanding duty, Francis, though none guessed it, was fatally stricken with what used to be known as galloping consumption and would die of it within three months. Will-power and sheer guts kept him going nearly to the end.

Francis said it appeared doubtful that any more Dakotas would fly in; the Japanese, massing in the jungle near Mawlu, were expected to attack that very day at dusk. About the future movement of our own columns – now, evidently, unlikely to land by air at White City – he could tell me nothing. Meanwhile, added Francis, I must find shelter for my men and make them dig.

By midday we had been provided with reserve posts, half-dug, within the defences of a South Staffordshire platoon on the side of a hill overlooking the White City light-plane strip which, unlike the much longer Dakota landing ground, had been sited within the perimeter in a re-entrant. The Africans, borrowing picks and shovels, began to deepen weapon pits, encouraged by Steve Elvery and Sergeant Speak while Nobby Hall and I lay idly smoking, sleepy after the tensions and anxieties of the last forty-eight hours. With half an ear we listened to the thud of picks against earth, the hot summer buzz of flies, snatches of talk and laughter from the English soldiers.

Some time later, the sun still well up, we heard a distant belch from jungle near Mawlu. The sound was immediately succeeded by by loud shouts of 'take cover', talk killed abruptly and in five seconds every South Staffordshire soldier hidden in his weapon pit. The Africans' holes, if still lacking overhead cover, were by now deep enough to afford them some kind of protection, but neither Nobby, Steve, Speak nor I had had wit enough to scrape the shallowest of shelters and leapt into a wide and unsavoury rubbish pit half-full of discarded ration tins. The rush of the projectile – whatever it might be – grew louder and louder as it fell out of the sky and we clung together, faces pressed against stinking dirt as the first detonation broke the afternoon into pieces. I could feel the bodies of my companions simultaneously relax: we looked at one another, rubbing filth and earth from our mouths, only to lie prone and taut again when we heard above us the swish and rustle of the second bomb.

For more than an hour 5.9 inch mortar bombs exploded amid the trees and scrub, a high proportion falling within close range. Our backs would be showered with stones and soil and lumps of hot metal hum, buzz and whine about the hill like swarms of demented bees. While my body seemed to disintegrate, my mind soon learnt to forecast with accuracy the likely destination of each missile by the pitch and volume of its descending voice, apprehension rising to a crescendo when a loud, feathery sort of wail announced one bound to burst close to our rubbish hole. Half-stunned though I might be by near misses, fear would at once be succeeded by

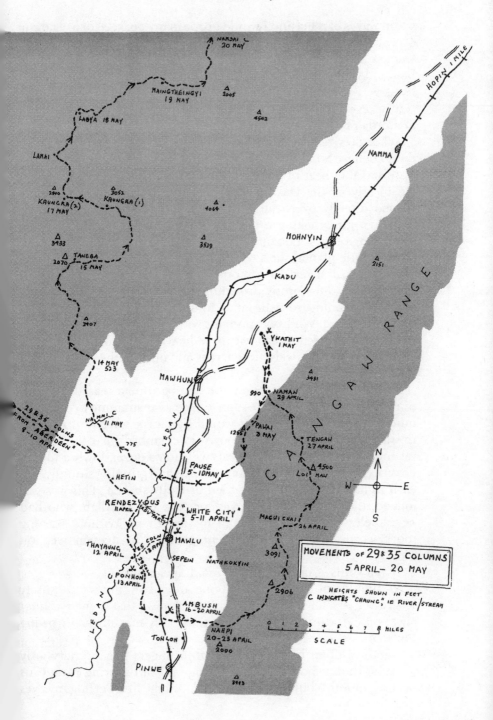

NARSAI C
20 MAY

MAINGTHEINGYI
19 MAY

△ 2005

LABYA 15 MAY

△ 4542

LAMAI

NAMMA

△ 2840          △ 3052
KAUNGRA (2)    KAUNGRA (1)
17 MAY

△ 4064

△ 3433                △ 3529

△ TANGBA
2070   15 MAY

MOHNYIN

△ 2151

△ 2407

KADU

14 MAY
523

YWATHIT
1 MAY

MAWHUN

△ 3431

29 & 35 COLNS
FROM "ABERDEEN"
9-10 APRIL

NAMMI C
11 MAY

990          NAMAN
              29 APRIL

775

1255   PAWAI
       3 MAY

TENGAW
27 APRIL

HETIN

PAUSE
5-10 MAY

△ 4500
LOI MAW

RENDEZVOUS
11 APRIL

"WHITE CITY"
5-11 APRIL

MAGUI CHAI
26 APRIL

THAYAUNG
12 APRIL

35 COLN
13 APRIL

MAWLU

△ 3091

SEPEIN          NATAKOKYIN

MOVEMENTS of 29 & 35 COLUMNS
5 APRIL – 20 MAY

U PONHON
13 APRIL

△ 2906

HEIGHTS SHOWN IN FEET
C INDICATES "CHAUNG", IE RIVER/STREAM

AMBUSH
16-20 APRIL

NAHPI
20-23 APRIL

TONLON

0 1 2 3 4 5 6 7 8 MILES
SCALE

△ 2000

PINWE

△ 2913

LEDAN C

GANGAW RANGE

LEDAN

warm waves of relief and I would grope in my pockets for a cigarette – cigarettes, at dangerous or critical moments, creating for the smoker and those about him the comforting illusion that all must be well. After a while a troop of 25 pounder guns, those unloaded by Steve's men from Dakotas the night before, fired a few rounds in return, every shell loudly and ironically applauded by the South Staffordshire from their foxholes.

When Steve Elvery announced that aircraft were approaching we didn't believe him but a moment later all of us could distinguish the unmistakable beat of engines. First a stick of small bombs burst harmlessly by the Dakota strip; next the Japanese Zero fighters rushed directly overhead a hundred feet above the trees, their machine guns making a curious distant tearing sound, like the screeching of jays. Looking up, I caught sight of five snub-nosed, shapely little planes, their wings, marked with red suns, gleaming like tarnished silver. In a moment they had gone, the crash of Japanese mortar bombs drowning all sound of their departure. Machine-gunning from the air we found much less frightening than being mortared. While weapon pits with thick overhead cover gave reasonable protection against these heaviest of mortar bombs, a shallow excavation twelve feet across and open to the sky provided little indeed.

At six o'clock in the evening the bombardment ceased. For two minutes there was complete silence, every ear straining to catch the innocent-sounding thud that would signal the advent of another missile. When we heard voices above us we climbed out of the rubbish pit and stretched ourselves, as cats will after a doze, slowly and lux-uriously, shaking dirt from our uniforms and grinning stupidly. No African had been killed, wounded or badly shaken. This was war indeed, they muttered, such violence the will of Allah, who had nevertheless been good enough to save them. Without wasting more words our men began energetically to deepen weapon pits.

'What's this – are you afraid?' said Speak, teasing.

'Certainly not, sargie,' replied one, offended. 'But we are surely of greater use alive than dead? Allah knows that a man cannot always be fortunate. And then those sky-machines, throwing bullets!'

Garaba Gonari brewed tea, his thin fingers playing nervously with the leather-bound amulets hanging from a string round his neck as, mouth a little open, he stared into the fire. Feeling my eyes on him he looked up smiling, teeth brilliant against plum-dusky lips.

'It is nearly ready, sir. The water bubbles.'

'What did you think of the Japan mortar bombs, Garaba?'

He giggled, a dark shadow creeping upward from his neck indicating a blush.

'I was much afraid,' he answered in his slow voice. 'I covered my face with my hands and lay like one dead.'

'And now?'

'Now I feel better, master. Allah has taken away the fear that was within me.'

Nobby Hall and I, assisted by Garaba and by Nobby's orderly, lost no time in digging a pit to share. When it had become deep enough to stand up in we laid branches across the coffin-shaped slit-trench, covered them with layers of parachute silk (easily picked up) and shovelled a foot's thickness of earth on top, leaving uncovered space enough to give us elbow room to lean against the parapet and point our weapons. For a touch of luxury, we lined the bottom of the trench with a carpet of yellow silk.

Gradually the sky was drained of colour, the sun sinking into the forest trees after gilding for a moment the wing of the broken glider on the far side of the Dakota strip. We waited.

Precisely at the hour Francis Stuart had predicted, just on dark, a storm of machine gun and mortar fire burst from the southern side of the block to announce that the Japanese had begun their attack. There followed a tremendous noise, explosions of Japanese artillery shells and mortar bombs almost drowned in competition with the bangs and crumps of ours, the more dignified, deeper voices of Vickers and Bren readily distinguishable from the hysterical screech of the rapid-firing enemy light machine guns. Punctuating all these we could hear continuous rifle shots and crashes of grenades, while every few seconds one of our 2 inch mortar parachute flares, dropping very slowly out of the sky, would shed over trees and undergrowth and wire a beautiful, unearthly orange radiance. Nobby and I stood against our parapet, peering nervously ahead and fingering Stens. If in no imminent danger, we imagined that at any minute we might be. But our slope was not attacked; the perimeter wire against which the Japanese bravely hurled themselves guarded the southern flank of a hillock a hundred and fifty yards away. Even when we realised this we couldn't relax, the battle too close and too real and we new. And what if the enemy should break through? I remembered training pamphlets warning us against Japanese infiltrators disguised as bushes, and looked fearfully around me whenever a flare went up.

By midnight two or three separate attacks had been beaten off and shooting slackened. We had seen no Japanese soldier, plain or camouflaged, and in spite of an earlier resolution to keep watch by turn until dawn, as one man Nobby and I slumped exhausted to the bottom of our trench, wrapping ourselves up in the yellow silk cloth against growing chill. I rummaged for the bottle of spirits I had brought from Assam in my pack and we took a generous swig each before falling asleep.

Violently awakened at three in the morning when the mortar hurled over the first of another series of bombs, scarcely breathing I lay still in the darkness, listening for the wobbling, long-drawn-out rustle and succeeding crash. The last drops of courage rushed from my heart.

'Charles, are you awake?' Nobby's voice seemed to come from miles away.

'Of course I'm bloody well awake!'

'Hope you're feeling as windy as I am.'

'Windier, I should think. Where's that bottle?'

We swallowed several mouthfuls each; never had I needed a drink so badly and the warmth of the rum worked wonders, dutch courage unquestionably better than none. I tried to picture the enemy mortar crew. They would be small men with unreadable faces, well-trained, devoted. I saw them sliding the five foot bomb down the barrel, putting hands over ears as it rushed out, waiting expectantly to hear the distant crump. I dozed off, then fell into deep sleep.

Garaba waked me with a mug of tea well after dawn. Daylight, blue sky, the living faces and voices around me: everything I saw and heard seemed preternaturally vivid and beautiful. I wanted to shout, to sing and cheer.

That day we dozed again in the sun, drinking many mugs of tea and listening to stories of the earlier fighting told us by Yeomans, the ginger-bearded South Staffordshire platoon commander whose defensive area we shared. For officers and men of this distinguished battalion, White City and the Henu battle – that fought before the block could be established -- proved but a beginning. They went on with Calvert to Mogaung, after its capture few indeed remaining on their feet: Yeomans ( I was glad to hear many years later) one of this minority.

There remained time and to spare for introspection. In the fore-front of my mind stood the question of whether I should be able to master fear – terror, even – when under fire, threat of fire or actual physical assault. Fear kept on leash is natural and freely admitted; men quite nerveless – they do exist – rare phenomena. But fear uncontrolled, fear which paralyses action or becomes rampant, is another matter, as having listened to many a true tale I well knew. Dismaying and ugly, it leads private soldiers to endanger their mates and reduces officers to a state of pitiable ineptitude. If after the event attitudes may soften somewhat, in the heat of fighting there can be neither time nor room for sympathy with those stricken: at best an embarrassing encumbrance, at worst they menace the safety of all near them, like a mortal contagion.

It happened that common physical courage, or nerve, was a quality I had always conspicuously lacked. At school and Sandhurst, for example, I had been compelled to steel myself even when faced with a gymnasium vaulting horse and often flunked the leap. To list my many phobias, which included soccer, riding and flying, would be as depressing as irrelevant; but since one could scarcely exist in a closed society of vigorous young men and be known for a poltroon, I had learnt by experience how to conceal the more obvious manifestations of cowardly timidity and could only hope that professional training and sense of responsibility would outweigh involuntary terrors, or at least allow me to come to terms with them.

Each of the days we spent in White City resembled the first. There would be attacks, in varying degrees of ferocity, every night from the east and south-east, but they failed to pierce through the thick coils of rusting wire and heaps of Japanese corpses lay putrefy-ing by them. An all-pervading stench of corruption hung in the air; myriads of flies tormented us. The great mortar, said to be German and of First World War date, continued to scourge; known as the 'coal-scuttle', it had an evil effect on the White City garrison. The huge noise produced by its exploding missiles and the crazy whine of the metal lumps into which they disintegrated remorselessly attacked our nerves. We knew neither when a bombardment might begin nor when it would end.

In the darkness Dakotas, flying low, dropped rations and ammunition and also medical supplies for the makeshift underground casualty station, containers crashing through trees and banging against slopes. Many would be caught up in branches and daylight reveal scores of parachutes hanging limp and pallid on the treetops, like linen hung out to dry – perfect aiming marks for the Japanese guns. American light-planes, buzzing dark-green dragonflies, carried the wounded and seriously ill to hospitals in India. Twisting over the trees, they would touch down on the strip just in front of the Nigerian party's foxholes, and having pulled up would wheel round, taxi as far as the Dannert wire and there wait impatiently until stretchers could be fixed in position for lying casualties and bandaged 'walking wounded' be gathered safely aboard. As soon as their passengers were inside the light-planes would race along the grass for a couple of hundred feet before springing into the air with the agility of mallard from a pond.

Bombers and fighter-bombers from Wingate's private, all-American Air Commando frequently attacked the nests of Japanese in the forest concentration areas whence they deployed to assault White City. If there were no mortar fire to anchor us we would stand on the hillocks watching. Sailing over at 10,000 feet, small and black like flies, the fighters would circle their targets, gradually losing height; then, one after another, peel off and dive steeply, swift as stooping peregrines. We could see the bombs, like toys at that distance, falling from their wings, brown clouds of soil and smoke erupting above the treetops well before the 'whoomph' of the bursts could reach our ears. After emptying their machine guns into the debris the fighters, sunlight winking on their backs, would spiral away, reform and return to their base in India. Medium bombers, Mitchells, ponderous as flying stag-beetles, cruised slowly along in level flight, releasing clusters of white parachute bombs which floated down as gently as dandelion seeds on a still day. As soon as the parachutes touched earth the bombs would explode in a succession of loud grunts, shaking the White City hills.

I visited Brigade Headquarters often, vainly seeking news of our mislaid columns from Francis Stuart, and on one such visit to the excavations and sandbags of the White City nerve-centre met Brigadier Michael Calvert for the first time.

Wingate's disciple from the days of our Burma defeat, Calvert had been a column commander in the 1943 Chindit expedition and had proved himself as enterprising and bold as during the earlier and doomed campaign when Burma was forfeited. Already he had a great name; now that Wingate had been killed, Calvert in the eyes of many Chindits – certainly in those of his own brigade – his natural successor in the field. A regular sapper officer in his early thirties, powerful, stocky, short-necked, low-browed and with stamina apparently inexhaustible, the brigadier, his face battered in the boxing ring, could be confused with nobody. He possessed a magnetic rather than flamboyant personality. There was nothing consciously showy about Calvert; he remained entirely natural, his talk at times rambling and difficult to follow. In the middle of giving battle orders to assembled column commanders (delivered in a conversational rather than peremptory tone) the brigadier, disconcertingly, would always be capable of breaking off to speak of birds, his life at Cambridge or other equally irrelevant topic. Once I heard him stop in mid-sentence, lost in thought, then recover himself to say:

'Which was I talking about, men or mules?'

Brigadier Calvert was a highly imaginative man, and though occasionally moody or irritable his personal courage, his resource and resolution had already become Chindit bywords. Enriched by an outstanding gift for leadership, a gift impossible to analyse, Calvert as a commander had no peer. His praise was music.

One morning I saw our own Brigadier Gillmore, accompanied by Chris Harrison, stepping out of a light-plane and lost no time in scrambling down the hill to intercept Chris. What was going on, what had happened to the battalion? Both columns, he said, had been flown to Aberdeen, a Chindit stronghold fifteen miles to the west, as yet unharried, poor flying conditions having delayed and disorganised departure from Assam and a complete platoon of No 35 Column, some support weapons and many mules left at Lalaghat. Peter Vaughan, according to Chris, was now tramping with the battalion along jungle tracks towards White City and should arrive that same day, or at latest the next.

'Well,' I said, 'thank God for some news. But what the hell are you doing here?'

'I was hooked for brigade-major just after you left – Gordon Upjohn's gone to the 6th. I did my damnedest to get out of it, but it wasn't any good.'

'What about the column?'

'You've got it now.'

Flown in several days ahead of ours, the 6th Nigeria Battalion, marching towards Aberdeen from the base established by Calvert's gliderborne brigade, had had the misfortune to be ambushed in darkness when crossing the railway line and in the confusion partly dispersed. Its commanding officer was sent back to India and Upjohn, the original brigade-major, promoted in his place to pull things together.

The news that I was destined to lead No 29 after all scarcely
touched me. It didn't sink in, the physical absence of the column
itself making it a no more than theoretical prospect. But I did spare
a thought for Chris; it was cruel luck to have had his command
snatched away as soon as taken over. A brigade-major, however
brilliant, must live in the shadow of his brigadier.

Peter Vaughan and the battalion failed to turn up that day, the
next or the next but one. No wireless message had been received from
him, nor could any be got through. Very anxious, I feared disaster.
It had overtaken the 6th Battalion and we might well have fallen victim
ourselves. Meanwhile Gillmore took over command of White City
from Calvert; the 12th Nigeria Battalion, more than holding its
own, had been manning a sector of the defences for some days. I
was sitting on a sandbag in the Brigade Headquarters dugout chatting to Chris when Jerry Bladon, the reconnaissance platoon commander of No 35 Column, made a sudden and dramatic entry. I
stared at him, heart pounding. A survivor from massacre? But two
Nigerians followed Jerry, both of whom smiled widely in greeting.
Rout was improbable.

Jerry Bladon said that Peter Vaughan lay doggo in teak forest six
miles to the west with both columns. Listening, with some
apprehension, to nightly battles and daily bombardments from the
White City direction, Peter had had no means of knowing whether
the place might be held by Chindits or Japanese, all his wireless sets
having unaccountably failed, and therefore sent Jerry to discover
the outcome before venturing his command closer to the block. On
Peter's part a very prudent step, it must have been a hair-raising
experience for Jerry Bladon, who even had he known that White
City held firm could still have had no idea where the investing
Japanese concealed themselves. One is hard put to it to imagine circumstances in conventional warfare in which a totally inexperienced
platoon commander could be entrusted with so dangerous and
important a first assignment. Jerry had done well.

' – and thank God I'm still in one piece,' he said. 'From the way
these chaps in White City blazed away at us you'd have thought
we'd been wrapped in Jap flags. This was my third shot at getting
inside the wire!'

Brigadier Calvert now intended to collect together a number of
columns and lead them south and east against the Japanese infantry
and artillery assembled in the Mawlu and Sepein areas, hoping by
diversionary attacks to reduce enemy pressure on the block itself.

Our own 7th Battalion, instead of helping to defend White City, as originally planned, was to form part of Calvert's striking force.

It followed that my redundant advanced party ought as soon as possible to rejoin the battalion, and accompanied by Jerry Bladon, Nobby and I and Steve Elvery's platoon heaved packs into position and crossed the wire barrier. We had lived in White City for just over a week and felt mightily relieved to escape from the shells, coalscuttle mortar bombs and stench of Japanese bodies. Now, nervously as well as laboriously, we found ourselves trudging away from the block and across the empty Dakota landing strip in the heat of the day. My equipment seemed to weigh a ton and already I dripped with sweat. At White City, lolling about on the hills or crouching in foxholes, we had become softer than for months past and in the open paddi felt visible and defenceless. Ahead of us stood an endless wall of sombre, close-ranked trees, and having gained their cover we sat down by a stream to ease backs and smoke. Clear shallow water gurgled over a stony bed; Shan women were washing clothes and bathing. Two or three of the younger and more attractive of them looked anxious. Taking up our loads, struggling with webbing straps, we lurched to our feet again after the brief halt and with Jerry and his two henchmen as guides plodded for the first time through the quiet Burma forest. Sunlight filtered through only in narrow shafts, freckling tree boles and the big dead leaves underfoot; but these trees, mostly teak, though of fair height scarcely bore comparison to the sky-scraper sort we were later to come across high in the Kachin hills astride the valley.

Dusk was threatening to overtake us when a concealed sentry's loud challenge brought hearts to mouths. We stopped dead: simultaneously a black face appeared from behind a tree trunk.

# CHAPTER 11

# Ambush

As Peter, Dicky Lambert and others gathered round us in the rapidly fading light I felt enormously relieved to see the faces of friends and companions again, however quiet our reunion. We from White City were regarded as experienced men: had we not been shelled, heard and seen shots fired? Steve's Nigerians would undoubtedly have taken every advantage of their temporary eminence; I wish I could have overheard the stories they must have told.

The place of rendezvous appointed by Calvert for his striking force lay only a few miles from Peter's bivouac and we reached the spot early the following morning. To the east were some dry, fallow paddi fields and No 29 Column pioneer officer superintended a hundred men as they levelled the low banks separating field from field, their object to make a landing strip for Calvert's light-plane, due to arrive that afternoon. I strolled over to watch the Africans slashing away with matchets, their faces and bare arms black against the paddi's faded green. Water buffaloes peacefully grazed, smoke from a nearby village crawled into the sky, a cock crowed. The Burma air smelt aromatic, cleaner, fresher than the powerful conglomerate of Indian smells which had captivated my youthful imagination. The whole scene struck me as one of profound tranquillity, violence here unthinkable, an outrage, the country too beautiful to be trampled and fought over by alien armies.

When Calvert's plane landed an officer of ours escorted him to the battalion's patch of jungle and he formally welcomed British leaders and those few African NCOs who understood English. The brigadier spoke simply, without employing one of the narcotic platitudes usually adopted by red-tabbed officers, and finished by saying how honoured he felt to have us under command. Sincerity shone through his words like a light. The little speech, striking exactly the right note, heartened us all.

Conscientiously elaborate preparations for our first Burma supply drop were set in train just on dark. The result was disappointing. The long, L shaped line of beacon bonfires was lit as soon as the throb of

approaching aircraft could be heard and we waited in some excitement, straining our eyes to distinguish navigation lights from stars
before flashing skyward the recognition letter, but though an
answering wink reassured us nothing would persuade the Dakotas
to fly lower than three thousand feet, too high for a concentrated
drop. As a result the parachutes, like confetti thrown from a child's
fist, were scattered at random over a square mile of jungle.

After stuffing what we had managed to salvage of the cartons of
American 'K' rations into packs, pouches and haversacks, we joined
Calvert's long procession of soldiers and mules wending south.
Dead teak leaves, large and crisp, cracked like pistol shots beneath
our boots and every time the Lancashire Fusilier column ahead of
mine happened to pause the Africans gripped their rifles tightly
and peered apprehensively between the trees. It was dusk when we
reached the village, Thayaung, selected by Calvert from the map as
the base from which to launch his attacks and which it was our particular business to hold safe. We found it deserted.

In all likelihood not an enemy breathed within a mile; but as
soon as I began my reconnaissance of No 29's allotted defensive sector
a wave of near-panic all but drowned me. Alone in the undergrowth
except for Garaba, I suddenly, and quite irrationally, felt paralysed
with dread of a Japanese surprise attack before we had organised
ourselves to meet it. The reconnaissance itself, presenting no problems, was the kind of thing carried out on countless training exercises,
and when I had finally managed to pull myself together well
enough to complete the job to my satisfaction I gave orders to my
waiting officers. The various groups confidently and quietly settled
in as a matter of routine, nobody, I hoped, having observed my
private battle. But I felt all too conscious of the fact that as No 29
Column commander I had in literal truth made a very shaky start.

Long bars of dark cloud striped a green sky at dawn (a picture
clearly recalled) as the British and Gurkhas of Calvert's force moved
east to find and attack their objectives, which included the area
from which it was believed the coalscuttle belaboured White City.
Our own two columns, as unproven, were left in reserve to hold
Thayaung as base and Dicky Lambert and I sat under a tree discuss-
ing Calvert's plan. Dicky had inherited Z Company from me and
would discover for himself what I had already learnt training in
India: since its one swollen rifle company constituted the column's
fighting nucleus, a Chindit company commander could be left little
or no scope for independent action. The four rifle platoon officers

joined us; Steve and Blossom Eede talkative and exuberant; Tich Cooper, small, grim and knowing, contradicting flatly everything they said; Denis Arnold listening to and laughing at him.

I remembered the photograph taken at Ibadan of Z Company officers; we sat formally on chairs and wore Sam Browne belts, shining boots and shorts immaculately creased. I have a copy still. Dicky Lambert, scowling, seems to squint, Denis looks serene, Steve grins inanely and Tich, sitting bolt upright, has crossed his legs in such a manner as to convert him from the shortest to the tallest of us (he had learnt the trick at school, he told me at the time). Thousands of miles from Ibadan now, our boots dull and scratched, our clothing dirty, unkempt and stale with sweat, we used the same sort of catchphrases and the younger men laughed nearly as often if more quietly. Yet already we had altered in a way hard to define or even to discern. We had become tenser, like wild creatures perpetually on the qui vive, watching and listening for inimical sound or movement.

Later that morning Calvert required a company to attack Mawlu. Peter Vaughan, seizing his first chance of action with both hands, went off with Nobby Hall's. Half an hour afterwards I was instructed to put troops into Ponhon, a village a mile across the paddi. It had been occupied at dawn by men of 45th Reconnaissance Regiment who, after killing the few Japanese to be found, had moved on against more important targets. The village was to be held for the rest of the day as a firm leg on the ground forward of Thayaung.

Fussily I sited each rifle platoon myself, giving Dicky Lambert unnecessary early notice of what he might be in for. Subdued life flickered in Ponhon, after a while timid women emerging from shuttered houses and brown children appearing from nowhere to gaze in wonder at the African faces. The Shan women, shy but placatory, brought us potatoes, melons and red and green tomatoes like little rubber balls. Fowls scratched and clucked in dusty corners; the air became drowsy with flies. From the lantana undergrowth towards the railway line we could hear machine gun fire and mortars and see the grey drift of smoke above the forest.

Wounded Gurkhas began to straggle into the village by twos and threes. An aid-post had been established in a house near my headquarters and there casualties could be patched up before being sent across the paddi to Thayaung and flown out from the light-plane strip levelled that morning. We managed to commandeer bullock carts to take back the worst cases. All afternoon a trickle of soldiers came in, pale young men with blank eyes and empty faces, their wounds bound with field dressings stained with blood. Some of them hobbled in supported by friends more mobile, others were carried to the aid-post on stretchers made from bamboo and groundsheets. Removed from the excitement, the hot confusion of battle, the little wounded Gurkhas looked defenceless and puzzled, like hurt children.

The shadows of houses and trees lengthened, the sun sank. The women disappeared within doors and with the dark I became a little nervous. Since every tomato had been eaten long since, hunger began to nudge us; we had left packs at Thayaung.

At 10 o'clock a galloper from Brigade Headquarters brought a message ordering withdrawal, and Dicky sent off runners to warn his rifle platoons. When all had assembled ready to move back to Thayaung I began to lead the way over the paddi, but hadn't shuffled a hundred yards before a second galloper appeared out of the night to countermand the order. Cursing, Dicky gave directions for platoons to return to their original positions. There was some confusion, men stumbling against one another in the darkness as each section of nine or ten soldiers picked its way as best it could through a maze of paths and houses to its separate post. Irritated by this reversal of plan, I waited outside the village with Sergeant Major Kitt to make sure that the latest order had been understood and acted upon.

Suddenly, and from very close at hand, we heard a burst of Bren fire, one rifle shot and two grenade crashes. Instantly we turned into statues, staring into the darkness and expecting to hear more shooting, yells and running boots. The African sections couldn't yet be back at their post; many of the men would be walking through the village and Z Company highly vulnerable. I stood glued to the pathway, heart hammering. There was silence: not a footfall nor snapping twig.

'Better get back, sir,' whispered Kitt. We tiptoed up the path to the fenced compound I used as headquarters to find it crawling with very nervous Africans, bayonets fixed. Drage, a 45th Reconnaissance officer left with me by his column for some reason I cannot remember, had taken charge in my absence.

'What happened?' he asked.

'No idea. Seemed to come from a chap called Eede's platoon area.'

'Japs may have heard us moving out. Or seen us.'

'Unless some idiot's shot up his own section.'

We had no 'walky-talky' radios yet; no means of communication within the column existed except for runner, and I wasn't going to dispatch one that night even if he could have found his way. Every soldier would be on edge, a runner probably shot. We waited, still tense, but nothing further developed. In our packs at Thayung were blankets as well as rations and without them it became too cold for any but fitful sleep.

At dawn we heard a single shot. It had a hollow ring to it, like one fired from a revolver. A few moments later Blossom appeared, the rich bloom covering his cheeks like rouge displaying itself in startling patches, like a disease.

'Couldn't let you know last night, sir. Didn't know myself. It was too dark to see anything and the platoon jumpy as hell.'

Blossom Eede, recently from England, knew very little Hausa.

'Well?'

'There are two dead Japs in my platoon area. I've just seen 'em. One was still alive and I made a grab at him. The bastard tried to throw a grenade so – that was the shot you must have heard, sir. They got my best corporal last night. We're burying him now.'

'Who was it?'

'Ibrahim Maiduguri. Head and chest, grenade. Can't make out exactly what happened, sir. I think the Japs tried to sneak in when we left and got caught by Ibrahim leading back his section. The Bren gunner got both Japs all right but they seem to have been blown up by their own grenades, too. Awful mess they're in.'

It was full daylight now, everything quiet. This, I thought, would be a useful opportunity to allow some of the NCOs a first look at their enemy, knowledge that two Japanese had been killed for one African a bonus that might prove of psychological benefit. A party was collected and Blossom Eede led us to a patch of open ground between houses. There in the dust sprawled the bodies. One, still grasping in his right hand the grenade which he had tried with his ebbing strength to throw at Blossom, had a left arm ending in a bloodless, spongy stump from which bone protruded; his lips were drawn back from his teeth, as though in death he snarled. The other corpse lay face down, one leg bent sharply at the knee, coiled entrails, covered by a light film of dust, spilling into the sand. The face we could see was white as paper, without trace of yellow pigmentation. Except for this surprising pallor, the Japanese corpses looked much as imagination's eye had pictured them and my first close view of violent death elicited neither shock nor disgust. Yet the husks of men lying there must have printed on my mind so strong a pictorial impression that today I can recall every detail.

Upon the Z Company African sergeant-major the sight of the two enemy bodies had an unforeseen and pitiable effect. He stood rigid, motionless as the dead at whom he stared, unable to turn away, his lower lip trembling as a child's when tears are close, his eyes filled with a revulsion, horror and fear he couldn't hide. On the barrack square the man had roared like a bull, juniors lived in awe of his imposing presence. Now the sergeant-major found himself defeated before he had well begun by whatever spectre his first encounter with battle's handiwork had raised; and for the rest of the campaign he behaved like a drugged man, functioning only as a figure-head, Dicky and I careful not to provide him with an opportunity to fail explicitly.

At four in the afternoon, two days after Z Company had been withdrawn from Ponhon, the whole fighting strength of No 29 Column lay in ambush.

Marching from the west, the battalion had earlier crossed the railway line running close to and parallel with the road blocked fifteen miles to the north – with the railway – at White City. Peter Vaughan and I, leaving both columns hidden in dense jungle between railway and road, had crept with a small escort to that unmetalled and dusty artery and cautiously crossed it to look for an ambush position. Every soldier in the battalion must have heard the Japanese truck that clattered from north to south just after we had reached the railway; other motor vehicles from either direction might at any moment be expected.

On the day on which my own troops had done little of consequence at Ponhon the fighting by Calvert's British and Gurkha columns had, on balance, proved indecisive and failed to deflect the Japanese from aiming further blows at White City. A really successful action had been Peter Vaughan's attack on Mawlu, where all asked for had been accomplished and Peter very pleased with the way his Africans had fought in their first engagement. So were we all. No 35 Column had suffered about thirty casualties – mostly wounded, including a British platoon commander – Nobby Hall, my White City companion, having particularly distinguished himself. While Calvert prepared for a second attempt our battalion had orders to ambush any Japanese motor transport using the road, and Peter had given No 29 Column responsibility for the operation.

I hadn't searched long before picking out a slight eminence with a flattish top, almost leaning over the road. It was covered with bushes and a number of bare trees and just about large enough for our purpose. North of it, the road ran gently downhill for a hundred yards into a dip crossed by a narrow stream, then uphill for another fifty before disappearing over the brow. To cross the ford motor vehicles coming from the north would, I fancied, be forced to change gear and slow down. South of the low hill, or plateau, the road disappeared round a corner, but not so abruptly that we could be caught napping.

Peter had watched me, indeed almost stood over me, while I was examining the possible ambush site and given half a chance might have taken over; my Commanding Officer hated to be left out of anything promising action. I had thought it wise to forestall him if I could.

'Now, Peter – Colonel, sir! You told me this was to be my effort, so do let me find my own place. You've had your duffy at Mawlu and we've done practically damn-all.'

'All right, I know! But you ought to get a move on, Charles. What do you think of this spot?'

'I think it'll have to do. It's not bad. There's a track leading east into the jungle and I expect you'd like to have a look for a lay-back position somewhere along it for 35? Can I leave mules and soft stuff with you? I'll recce this properly and then get cracking.'

Peter had moved both columns across the road, my fighting elements staying close at hand but out of sight, ready to be placed in position. No 35 Column, together with my mules, wireless sets and other vulnerable bits and pieces had gone on into the jungle to establish a base or 'lay-back' about a quarter of a mile away.

And now we waited for something to turn up, sunlight hot on our backs. The Africans had made themselves scrapes to lie in, employing matchets, their all-purpose tool or weapon, looking something like a butcher's cleaver – scrapes hollowed out less for protection than concealment. The men with their various weapons – Vickers, Brens, rifles, Piats (shoulder-fired anti-tank guns) – lay along the edge of the little plateau in a rough semi-circle facing the road, ready to ambush traffic from either direction, the nearest black soldiers, no more than ten feet from the roadside, having been provided with generous numbers of grenades. There was opportunity now for me to take a look at the leafless trees, which had aroused my curiosity. In this green land, where foliage overflowed, so many standing naked were unusual. I found them to be unsuspected casualties of war, trunks scarred and pitted by bullets which, rather surprisingly, must have killed them. I wondered who could have fired these shots, and in what circumstances.

A jungle ambush, provided the intended victims put in their appearance, offered a more definite chance of success than any Chindit operation. Once the trap had been sprung and fire poured in, perhaps followed by the bayonet, the ambushing party could make itself scarce rather than await retribution. Ours, however, was not intended as quite of that sort; we had received no orders to fade away at discretion, come success or failure. In effect a road-block as well as ambush, it had to be maintained until Calvert gave the word for it to be abandoned.

As we listened for the sound of motor engines I could sense throughout the column considerable tension. I prayed for success, knowing that it would mean a great deal more to us than to the Chindit force as a whole; with the dice loaded in our favour, to botch things here might cast a gloom from which the Nigerians would be slow to recover. Their fighting spirit could, I suspected, be as quickly depressed as raised high.

Well over an hour had passed before we heard something approaching from the north. Near the road verge, just behind the half circle of listening men, stood one of the dead trees and I moved behind it, ready at the critical moment to release the Very light arranged as the signal for all who could see a target to open fire. The high whine grew louder and we could hear the rattle of bodywork jolting on the uneven road surface. Cautiously poking my head round the tree, I saw an open truck coming fast downhill towards the ford. Just as I had anticipated it slowed, the driver changing down to cross. Not until the lorry had reached a position opposite my tree did I intend to fire the Very pistol, but its front wheels had barely touched the stream before the loud bang of a Piat from the bushes near my feet all but deafened me. The anti-tank bomb exploded on the road our side of the ford in a great shower of sparks and at once six men tumbled out of the truck and ran for their lives up the hill, our bullets raising puffs of dust all round them. The Japanese, ludicrous in their terror, looked like brown scuttling beetles. Within a few seconds they had dodged into the trees and shooting stopped. Every enemy soldier had escaped.

'Who fired that Piat?' I shouted in Hausa. I was furiously angry and had every reason to be.

'Me. I did, sir,' said Tich Cooper from the bushes.

Having taken it for granted that the culprit must have been an over-excited African, I could scarcely credit my ears.

'You? What the bloody hell do you mean by letting off that thing before my signal?'

'It was slowing, we'd been spotted and I thought –'

'I don't give a damn what you thought! You're here to do what I tell you and now you've wrecked the whole thing! If ever you do anything like this again. . . .'

It was not an edifying scene and many Africans could overhear it. When I had calmed down a little Tich tried to persuade me that the driver had been about to turn round, but I remained convinced he had contemplated nothing of the sort. Another hundred yards and the truck would have been almost touching us: none of the six Japanese could possibly have escaped. Now our position was compromised, our chance surely gone. If anything came from the north after this it would be soldiers sent to dislodge us, not unsuspecting lorries; furthermore a mile south down the road lay a Japanese-occupied village, where the noise of our shooting must certainly have been heard. Vehicles approaching us through it would be bound to be warned.

A party of us walked down to have a look at the truck. Inside it we found carbines, notebooks meaningless to us but collected for Intelligence in India, one or two tins of petrol and several canteens of cooked rice still steaming. The rice may have been intended for friends in the village down the road; there was enough for two dozen men, as some lucky Nigerians discovered. Dicky Lambert drove the undamaged truck off the road and into the bushes, concealing it under cut boughs on the offchance that another would appear: Calvert's fertile brain might invent a use for what was undoubtedly the only vehicle in possession of his striking force. The brigadier himself crossed the road later that evening with fifteen hundred men, smiling when shown the camouflaged Japanese truck though less pleased when I had to report the premature springing of my ambush.

That night Dakotas circled and next morning Peter Vaughan sent men and mules to collect the battalion's share from Calvert's general supply drop. Peter had thoughtfully arranged for some wire to be dropped; I made my men stretch a concealed Dannert fence round most of the hill, not omitting to hide long coils in the lantana bushes on the far side of the road to impede enemy who might try

Nigerian Chindits climbing into the Dakota that will fly them into Upper Burma for operations. (IWM)

A Nigerian soldier, probably in the Arakan. His general appearance and filed teeth indicate a Tiv. (IWM)

Taken just prior to 77 Brigade's 'fly in' by glider. From left to right: Colonel Alison, USAAF; Brigadier Michael Calvert; John Barrow (Wingate's ADC); General Wingate, wearing his famous Wolseley helmet; Lt Colonel Walter Scott; Major Francis Stuart (Calvert's Brigade-Major).

to escape from ambush – if indeed ambush remained a possibility – in that direction. Should we be attacked, the wire as well as the deeper weapon pits that the soldiers now carved out with their matchets would help us defensively also.

Though I felt far from satisfied with the way things had gone up to now, others of the column seemed cheerful enough: Steve Elvery lively as a grasshopper, Sergeant Umoro Numan grinning and war-like, Sergeant Major Kitt prodigal with miscellaneous forecasts of disaster, some of which might, I thought, for once be near the mark. Calvert and his striking columns, after 'harbouring' for the night in jungle near No 35 Column, left the vicinity to tramp north for a second attempt against the enemy pounding White City, hoping this time to squeeze the Japanese up against the block itself. His British troops looked more weary than on the previous evening, their faces wearing the self-absorbed, almost furtive expressions of soldiers who know they are bound to be committed to battle that day.

Before the routine 'stand to arms' at dusk Peter Vaughan walked over to see us. The untidy stubble on his face, contrasting with his white forehead and outstanding nose, gave him a rakish appearance, like that of some well-born remittance man or gambler who, after losing his all, has dropped many rungs down the social ladder. Peter and I got on excellently. To a certain extent we complemented one another; he the impulsive commander, bold and almost without nerves, I the cautious adviser who tried to persuade him to temper impetuosity with prudence.

The Nigerians had began to buckle on equipment and stub out cigarettes preparatory to 'stand to' when Garaba Gonari quietly told me that he could hear motors in the north. We laughed at him, but I for one should have known better: if Garaba could find his way unerringly across strange country his ears might be supposed cap-able of detecting sounds that white men's could not. Suddenly other Africans were still and listening, but another minute had passed before their officers could themselves distinguish the unmistakable rumble of engines, faint at first but growing percept-ibly louder. I moved towards the road, throwing myself flat on the ground near the bare tree behind which Denis Arnold, very care-fully briefed, stood on duty with the loaded signal pistol. Within two minutes dusk became night. The volume of sound, growing harsher, suggested not one but a number of vehicles grinding towards us in low gear, my heart missed a beat or two when for a second I imagined I could detect the clatter of tank tracks. The convoy reached the top of the hill above the ford, loud Japanese exclamations now clearly audible. Several times the trucks halted with engines running, shouts coming from men on foot who, fearing a trap, must have been searching the road for mines. News of yesterday's abortive attempt had evidently spread. Suspense rose to a point almost beyond bearing as slowly, very slowly, the foreign voices and lurching trucks drew level with us, thirty feet from where I lay hidden among the leaves. For another ten seconds I heard only motor engines and the tramp of boots; then came a single urgent Japanese yell from the road. Looking up, I saw Denis raise his arm and loose the yellow light and on the instant every column weapon opened fire.

In so earsplitting a din one couldn't distinguish the voice of one kind of weapon from another. We lost ourselves in noise. By the time the shooting had slackened somewhat and I could make heard my 'cease fire' whistle signal, the leading truck was burning brightly with orange flames which cast flickering shadows, heat causing the roadside bushes to dance and sway. We could smell the pungency of burning rubber, the fire's breath warmed our cheeks and by its light I could see by the burning truck's front wheels two Japanese bodies lying half-entwined, like lovers. Moans issued from the darkness but exploding small arms ammunition, popping like squibs and sending wavering sparks into the night, soon drowned the voices of the dying men. Beyond the radiance shed by the flames the blackness was so dense as to appear solid. None of us could tell how many trucks stood riddled behind the burning leader.

By the glimmer of dawn I was near to persuading myself that the night's violence must have been hallucination or dream: this seemed like any other morning twilight in the jungle. Seeking reassurance I walked over to Dicky Lambert's pit, a few yards from mine. He smiled, climbed out of it and stretched.

'It was real, wasn't it?' I said. Dicky looked at me, his button eyes puzzled. He stood big and solid in the twilight, feet planted apart, a rifle over his shoulder.

'What was real, sir? I don't get it.'

'Last night, I mean.'

'My God, that was real enough,' he said. 'A bloody sight too real. What Japs are left will be lying up in the bushes, you bet. Trouble for somebody!'

'Probably for you, Dicky,' I told him. 'But I hope not too much.'

We walked to the edge of the perimeter and peered at the road. Though in the dim half-light one found it difficult to separate one from another, our impression was that five vehicles stood there nose to tail including the leading one, a twisted wreck still smoking.

As soon as the sky paled I sent out Dicky, Tich, Denis and thirty Nigerians to 'mop up' the area between our position and the ford on both sides of the road. So high a proportion of British would, I hoped, encourage soldiers new into action. The party crept away, fixed bayonets reflecting the grey sky, primed grenades stuck in belts, the Africans looking sleepy and apprehensive.

Almost at once rifle shots, grenade bursts and fire from Brens and Japanese light machine guns – easily distinguishable – could be heard from the undergrowth. I lay on my stomach in one of the scrapes on the perimeter attempting to follow events but saw nothing, though I could hear Dicky's voice shouting commands and ferociously urging on men inclined to hang back. Turning to say a word to the African lying in the scoop immediately to my right, I found he had that moment been shot through the forehead, killed either by a Japanese bullet or one fired by Dicky's Africans. What difference could it make to him, poor soldier?'

I was sweating with anxiety for officers and men when after half an hour Denis Arnold returned to ask for reinforcements. Unflurried, he might have been taking part in a routine training exercise.

'Japs all over the bloody shop, sir, taking pot shots from cover. Mostly wounded from last night. Got the chap next to me clean as a whistle – Shehu Godabawa. One Jap sat up, aimed at me and missed from ten feet! I saw him do it.'

Early on, Tich and his party had been observed crossing the road but after an immediate exchange of fire nothing had been heard from that direction since. Taking with him Sergeant Speak and another twenty Africans, Denis disappeared into lantana. Gradually the shooting diminished in volume, reports ringing out at longer and longer intervals. Yet these single rifle shots sounded more menacing than the earlier brisk exchanges; one felt they were coolly aimed at specific targets and couldn't tell whose shots they might be, ours or enemy's. Eventually there was a silence broken only by desultory African voices and Dicky Lambert emerged from the bushes, breathing hard. I could have embraced him. Some twenty Japanese had been killed by his party, he told me, besides those lying dead in the lorries, or near them, but Tich Cooper hadn't reported back. Dicky sat down on a log, lit a cigarette and yawned repeatedly.

'I'll go and look for Tich, I think I know where he went,' he said a moment later.

No sooner had Dicky spoken than Tich walked slowly towards us. He looked small and sick, hard to recognise as the perky, cock-sure soldier who carried a pack heavier than any and knew all the answers. He gripped the upper part of his right arm, his side and right sleeve dark with the blood which dripped steadily from his fingers to the ground, splashing with scarlet the dead leaves. Following slowly behind Tich came several Africans carrying awkwardly by shoulders and thighs a mortally wounded corporal, Abdullahi Fort Lamy, whose head already lolled. After lowering him to the ground at my feet his comrades gazed at him, murmuring sadly amongst themselves. The corporal sighed once and died. We helped Tich to a tree against which he could lean; someone lit a cigarette and put it between his lips.

'Jap got me through the elbow with a LMG burst. Two or three bullets. Smashed it properly. Right arm too. Abdullahi was hit in the belly by the same burst, poor sod. Well, boys, that's it.'

He couldn't raise a smile. Bitterly disappointed, Tich had burned for distinction and I believe would have achieved it.

I walked to the trucks. The sun shone, at the ford the little stream rushed merrily across the road. One Japanese vehicle appeared to be half full of dead and dying enemy whom Africans were dragging out and dumping on the road verge; they might have been handling so many sacks of refuse. Ordering my men to treat them more gently, I put a water-bottle to the mouths of those Japanese still showing flickers of life. A few opened black eyes to stare blankly, but most enemy still living had sustained desperate and ugly wounds and seemed beyond help, only three, in the opinion of Neil Leitch, my column doctor, being capable of survival. On my instructions the trio were carried up to our position on the hill by reluctant black soldiers at a loss to understand their commander's paradoxical wish to preserve the lives of foes. I was sternly warning them not to murder their prisoners when I heard a commotion behind my back and turned about. A Japanese NCO, taken for dead, had by some superhuman effort shaken off the hands lifting him from the truck and lunged at the nearest African with his bayonet. Now he stood upright in the back of the open lorry, face contorted, brandishing his weapon and shouting hysterically, his tunic stiff with caked blood. For a moment, before falling to Speak's pistol shots, the man appeared as one risen from the grave.

In front of the second truck lay a dead officer wearing polished leather leggings, a tall fellow with composed features who looked asleep. Getting an African to remove his sword and scabbard, I had them taken to my headquarters. (A large Japanese Rising Sun flag, a silk one, found in that officer's pocket hangs above the chimney-piece in my study, the solitary war trophy in my possession.)

Now that action seemed over I half-expected the usual white-armleted military umpires to appear, consult their notebooks and politely point out tactical errors, for the commission of which criticism might be expected from the exercise director when he presided over the conference for officers taking part as 'own troops' or 'enemy'. But this time four or five British rifles, surplus now, stood against a tree by Kitt's foxhole waiting to be disposed of. And there was blood on the road.

As many bodies as could readily be found of the twenty odd Japanese destroyed by Dick's party were dragged or carried to the side of the road to join the rest. We counted forty-one all told. My first idea, to bury them in two or three large pits, would have entailed hours of labour for soldiers without picks and shovels. It was asking too much of them, so I changed my mind; we would pile the corpses into one of the trucks and cremate them. Plenty of petrol was available and the selected vehicle began to burn vigorously, giving out clouds of nauseating smoke from which we fled. Expecting nothing but bones and ashes when the flames died, instead we found lumps of roasted, blackened flesh still recognizably human, grotesquely crowned with bleached steel helmets like inverted pots.

So far as I knew, none of us had felt in the least degree moved by the earlier spectacle of Japanese corpses lining the road like bundles of dirty washing. And now, whenever we had occasion to walk past the charred remains of men with white sticks for limbs, we were conscious of nothing but physical revulsion. They stank horribly.

The truth was that the Japanese, our enemy, the hobgoblins of the Burma forest, remained beyond the grasp of our imagination. We didn't hate them; they were too strange, too alien to hate. At times we hardly thought of them as men. Pitiless, inexorable, lacking (so we thought) all human warmth, giving no quarter and expecting none, the bodies we found often had fierce and scowling faces, without sign of the humanity that would have marked them kin. If Japanese officers indeed followed a code of conduct called 'Bushido', this code, its outward manifestations invisible, cannot have included rules for chivalry toward foes. For soldiers to surrender honourably in untenable situations has for centuries past been the military convention in Western warfare. In medieval days a knight taken prisoner had been accounted more valuable than a knight slain: a living man might be ransomed, his captors enriched. Since the Japanese soldier was heir to no such tradition, to be taken prisoner represented for him indelible disgrace; better the most appalling of deaths than that. However hopeless his position, no matter how severely he might be wounded, it was nearly unheard of for a Japanese fighting man to throw in his hand. To avoid capture he would unhesitatingly kill himself, or else allow himself to be killed, after making every effort to drag at least one of his enemy with him into darkness. We ourselves had already come across two examples of enemy mortally wounded determined to die fighting. When joined with their tenacity, hardihood and striking courage this ingrained attitude made the Japanese the most dangerous of opponents; and since we could neither comprehend nor equal it, we were inclined to dismiss the enemy's preternatural, indeed sometimes useless bravery and spirit of self-sacrifice as 'fanaticism'. Such a description let us out, so to speak: rational Europeans couldn't be expected to assume postures so uncompromising.

Yet the translations of captured enemy diaries printed in official intelligence bulletins failed to present the enemy soldier in the guise of fanatic determined only to kill or be killed. Without exception that I remember, the Japanese diarists struck the reader as homesick, hungry, maudlin and full of sensational despair; one would have said their collective morale must be at rock-bottom. It was difficult indeed to reconcile sentiments so gloomy with an unfailingly resolute demeanour in the field.

Perhaps four out of five carefully planned ambushes ought to suc-ceed. Nonetheless, as our first attempt too plainly showed, matters could well have gone awry. With every weapon cocked and ready, one black finger a shade too firmly bent about a trigger would have been enough to ruin the surprise upon which one depended. Out of scores, it needed only a single man to lose his head for confusion – panic even – to have followed; many soldiers are liable to become unsteady after nightfall at the best of times.

I decided to talk to all African NCOs who could be spared; they deserved praise. The men squatted on the dead leaves in a semi-circle round me while I told them I was proud of them and of the private soldiers whose example they set. It must have been a pompous little speech. Listening with serious eyes fixed on mine, now and again the sergeants and corporals would incline heads in acknowledgement as I reminded them that they should regard this as only a beginning; future actions would no doubt be more testing, casualties mount. They had seen for themselves the Japanese enemy, they knew the sort of men to be confronted. Was it not true that in no respect did they resemble Italian soldiers, or what they may have heard about them? Indeed, the NCOs admitted at last, it was certainly true, these 'Japans' were really fierce and wicked men. What a pity to keep any prisoners alive!

A quarter of a mile up from our hill, on the far side of the road, a light-plane strip had meanwhile been quickly levelled by men of No 35 Column, Blossom Eede with his platoon protecting it from interference next day as British, Gurkha and West African casualties waited for evacuation. The more lightly wounded, gathering in little knots on the road under our position, chatted together and smoked, entirely heedless of the stinking, half-cooked corpses in the burnt-out truck. Brigadier Calvert's men had returned at dark on the day following the ambush with some forty stretcher cases and sixty 'walking wounded'. After this second series of attacks White City would never again be assaulted. If the cost to his columns had been heavy, Calvert had succeeded in his aim. I hoped that he and his battle-weary men would feel heartened by the sight of five Japanese trucks standing derelict on the road.

Tich Cooper, who with other wounded had been looked after by Neil Leitch in No 35 Column's bivouac, dropped in to say goodbye. From his left hand swung the sword of the Japanese officer, which I had given him as a consolation prize; his Tiv orderly, crestfallen beside him, carried the blanket and the few personal things there could be found room for in the light-plane. Tich seemed a shade more cheerful now. Pretending to be envious of his wound and early return to India we pressed upon him the addresses of parents, wives and sweethearts and he promised to write to them and report our progress. It must have been Steve Elvery who suggested that when his arm mended Tich might like to apply for a vacancy as instructor on a Piat-firing course. When it was time for him to go

Tich strutted down the road on his way to the strip with a touch of the old swagger, flourishing the sword above his head in farewell.

I paid a visit to our Japanese prisoners before they too were whisked away to India. I had had a good look at one of them the previous day, a meek little man with an ingratiating smile filled with gold teeth who had smoked several of my ration cigarettes. Like Agag he had stepped delicately, but unlike that ill-fated monarch had not been hewn in pieces. One of the three had unfortunately died of his wounds. I write 'unfortunately' not because I felt particularly sorry but because creatures so rare were prized by Intelligence experts in India. Knowing that they would be barred forever from their homeland if ever they should be so stupid or so craven as to fall into the hands of the Emperor's foes, Japanese prisoners more often than not provided every scrap of information asked for.

Both survivors, lying in the shade on stretchers, watched every move I made as I approached them. Particularly observant was a Japanese soldier who, I thought, represented his comrades more truly than the feeble smoker who had dared to smile. This man's features remained immobile, his eyes expressionless – flies explored his face, but no muscle twitched – the whole of his attention concentrated on me, whom he appeared to recognize as the enemy commander. Perhaps he was trying to deduce from my attitude how soon his execution was likely to take place. The Nigerians all around him would certainly have demonstrated repeatedly and in unmistakable pantomime how he would end had they any say in the matter!

It occurred to me that when we left our road-block and moved to fresh woods a Japanese officer coming upon the roasted corpses of his compatriots might assume that a horrid atrocity had been perpetrated, that men had been burned to death while wounded but still living. It looked rather like it. Since Chindit prisoners were liable to receive short shrift, I had no wish to exacerbate matters. The Japanese propaganda machine might make capital out of this supposedly wicked act; dramatic photographs be taken, false descriptions disseminated. So I wrote in block capitals a notice on a piece of cardboard from a ration packet and stuck it on a conspicuous tree trunk by the road. It read:

TO THE JAPANESE COMMANDER

THE BODIES YOU SEE IN THE TRUCK WERE NOT BURNT ALIVE. THEY WERE PLACED THERE WHEN ALREADY DEAD AND THEN SET ON FIRE

(Signed) C. C. A. CARFRAE, MAJOR

With the remainder of Calvert's tired force Peter Vaughan with No 35 Column marched off to a valley near a village called Nahpi, four or five miles to the east. Glued to our road-block unsupported, we grew nervous and apprehensive of attack – at least I did – not understanding that the Japanese who had invested White City had shot their bolt and were at least as anxious as we to remove themselves from the vicinity. Patrols exchanged a shot or two, but no enemy transport attempted the road and this omission alone should have made it obvious that the Japanese had temporarily lost confidence: it was, we believed, the only route for miles that trucks could use. I happened to be on the perimeter one morning when a single Japanese scout was seen skulking between trees; seizing a rifle, I held him in the sights but after a second's hesitation didn't shoot. 'Might miss or wound and give away the position,' I thought to myself. It may have been the right choice. Our task remained the same, we were to ambush anything we could; and in spite of the wrecked lorries signposting our noisome road-block the enemy might have imagined that its occupants had gone.

In the small hours of the second night a sound roused Dicky Lambert. Though still half-asleep he could make out, looming over him, a figure wearing what he took to be a Japanese helmet. It was the rule in every column that no shooting inside the perimeter defences – unless of course they should be completely overrun – was permitted, for obvious safety reasons; but Dicky, convinced that in another moment he would be a dead man unless he acted, fired his revolver and scared the wits out of us all.

After a moment of dead silence the African column sergeant-major's voice came from the darkness. 'Sir, what have I done that you should shoot me in the arm?' Wearing a close-fitting woollen cap-comforter – in silhouette indeed resembling the Japanese type of steel helmet – he had been conducting a routine change of sentries. Very luckily, the bullet had barely nicked the flesh. I could hardly blame Dicky; every man of us had become as jumpy as he. This ludicrous incident, separated only by a hair's-breadth from tragedy, served to underline the wisdom of the rule Dicky Lambert had broken and to avoid future accidents I prohibited the wearing of cap-comforters after dark.

It came as a huge relief to abandon the bare trees and sickening smell of charred death when after two or three days Peter suggested to Calvert that we be withdrawn.

CHAPTER 12

# Raid on Ywathit

The valley in which Calvert's force rested was beautiful. Steep, thickly forested hills on either side raised shaggy heads and at their feet a clear-water amber brook rushed noisily through paddi fields towards the level jungle we had left behind. In the early morning shifting skeins and sheets of mist shrouded foothills already hazy with smoke from a thousand Chindit breakfast fires, above the mist, detached from earth, floating tall green hill-tops, islands planted in the sky overnight. The peace of the place sank into me; I forgot the troubled nights by the road and lying on my back under a bamboo canopy would watch the narrow leaves making patterns against the sky like Chinese brush-and-ink drawings on rice paper. Ever since the ambush I had felt unaccountably depressed as well as edgy.

Filthy by now, encrusted with reddish soil, I spent part of every morning on a rock in the stream scrubbing myself with a rapidly diminishing chunk of soap while Garaba, below, washed my shirt, trousers and over-ripe socks, humming in falsetto.

'This is fine country, Garaba. What do you think of it?'

'Perhaps! But there are no farms here, not real farms. Where are the crops? In Nigeria there is no shooting, nor Japans.'

'But, Garaba, I've told you many times the Japans do not live here. They have taken Burma – thieved it – from the King of England and from the people who live in the villages.'

'It is so. You have said it: it must be true. Here are clean socks. The others will dry this afternoon. Look at the fires on the hill! It is time to brew tea.'

This kind of talk held very little interest for Garaba. What concerned the Nigerians most was whether they felt dry or wet, warm or cold, replete or hungry, safe or exposed to danger.

Experts of various descriptions who had joined No 29 Column in India not long before the fly-in had by now become assimilated, contributing to our own special atmosphere or column spirit. Recent arrivals had included Fisher, my Burma Intelligence Corps officer, who brought with him three splendid Christian Kerens, and Corporal Sykes, our column wireless expert.

Captain Fisher, an Anglo-Burman schoolmaster of forty, by several years the oldest member of the column, his face unlined, resolute and sad, hated the war in Burma with a quiet intensity none of us could match and in his unobtrusive way showed exemplary fortitude and calm. His duties to question villagers and obtain information of the enemy, act as my interpreter and buy any food for the column he could persuade the inhabitants to sell, Fisher also insisted on joining patrols if there were a possibility of coming across Kachin or Shan and played a full part in defensive action. Anglo-Burmans, of whom I met several, make an ideal blend, seeming to inherit the best qualities of both parent races. Curiously, all spoke what in those days was called 'Oxford English' perfectly though none, I believe, had ventured further afield than India.

Corporal Sykes, a magician with wireless, belonged to the Royal Corps of Signals and did it honour. The layman is inclined to admire to an exaggerated extent the genuine expert in any field and be willing to credit him with more character and colour than he may deserve; but Sykes certainly possessed character. Deliberate in speech and movement, a bespectacled Yorkshireman with an earnest demeanour, he ruled his English-speaking Southern Nigerian operators with goodhumoured firmness but little faith in their skill, apparently preferring the mules that carried his sets, which he made much of. When none but sentries and probably the doctor would be awake and on duty Sykes would fiddle with his sets by the light of a shaded torch, showing never a trace of impatience no matter how long the message he struggled to get through in near-impossible conditions for wireless traffic. He rarely failed.

It is said that a soldier's recollections of war must always be distorted, that he will look back either with undue bitterness or false sentimentality, his comrades-in-arms, in retrospect, changing themselves into devils or angels; and I may paint my own in colours brighter than life. But I don't think so. The harshness of war may discover in men who appear perfectly ordinary qualities which, if likely to bury themselves again as soon as the first white flags are hoisted, remain no less fine and true on that account. Martial virtues are the dunghill's flowers.

Since our two columns were no longer required to defend White City, we remained with Brigadier Michael Calvert when he left Nahpi and moved north.

The battalion had encountered formidable hills on its initial march from Aberdeen, but until this climb I myself had met none but reasonably level jungle. Now we struggled up the hills of the Gangaw range, reaching up to 4,000 feet and so steep that we were compelled to pause every quarter of an hour to recover breath and longed to throw away those cursed packs. Moving along single-file tracks against the grain of the land, either we plodded towards summits we seemed never to attain or slithered down slopes so perilous that had a man lost his footing he might have tumbled straight into the rocky clefts far below. Down these combes rushed infant torrents on their way to join the rivers of the railway valley, the sun scarcely touching the lowest slopes where in sea-green twilight vegetation flourished in tangled skeins of dark and glossy leaves. Further up, where more light penetrated, grew bamboo clumps with canes thick as organ pipes, but near the hilltops the bamboo thinned and great trees stood evenly ranked, straight as telegraph poles and without a branch for sixty feet, their grey trunks, marvellously smooth, spreading out near the base to form buttresses with folds like garments carved in stone. In the leaf canopies, far above our tramping boots and full in sunlight, arboreal beasts, bright birds and insects without number pursued unseen their unimaginable lives.

From the crest of Moi Law, the highest summit of all, the view spread before us inspired such wonder that for a minute we forgot our weariness. For mile upon mile, stretching to the world's end for all we knew, jungle-covered hills lay in successive bronze-green folds, the flat paddi fields of the railway valley, invisible now through mist and cloud, another country.

An intelligence section Keren of Fisher's managed to procure two or three starved-looking chickens one evening from a village within earshot and I invited the Brigadier, Francis Stuart and Peter to share them. The menu also featured rice, a peculiar-tasting herb soup made by the Kerens, and a bottle of 'luxury drop' rum. Tearing apart the chickens with our fingers, in medieval great hall style, we devoured them with gusto. If more bone than flesh, they made a wonderful change from the perennial K Ration tins. (K rations, the lowest-scaled or 'hardest' American Army issue, to be used, according to US regulations, for no longer than three days at a stretch, represented our staple and normally only diet throughout the campaign, as I should earlier have mentioned.) We talked and drank rum well into the night, sitting in a glade on a mat of leaves, the air about us sweet with wood smoke. From the village we could hear Kachin voices and in the forest the high laughter of Nigerian soldiers. Calvert, alternately merry and ironic, said at one point that he should enjoy being in charge of the Irrawaddy flotilla after the war; at another that every high commander ought to nourish the sense of military history in most of them strikingly deficient, hence the strategic and tactical blunders they were so given to perpetrating.

By the fourth or fifth day after leaving Nahpi we found ourselves travelling downhill towards the jungle bordering the paddi fields of the railway corridor, though well north of White City. Uniformed Kachin levies armed with rifles began to flit along the trails. Coming and going mysteriously, they were, it appeared, members of an Intelligence network directed by a British officer, Musgrave Wood (in civil life a cartoonist), from a concealed base near Naman the Japanese had been unable so far to discover. Within a mile or so of this secret hideout a light-plane landing strip, serviceable in dry weather, had been created out of paddi and marshland. Four or five miles further north, and nearer to the railway, a fair-sized village called Ywathit, reported by the Kachin levies to be garrisoned by Japanese, attracted Peter's interest. It was rumoured that we should soon have to leave Calvert's force and my Commanding Officer, as usual eager for the smell of powder, proposed to make a farewell gesture by attacking the place. Calvert, not one to refuse an offer of this kind, agreed provided that Peter treated the project as raid rather than death-or-glory attempt to gain ground to no purpose. Resistance proving stiff, heavy casualties were to be avoided.

Peter insisted on taking with him Nobby Hall and me, plus a very small escort, to have a close look at Ywathit. It was, I believe, the old 'Field Service Pocket Book' that contained the memorable sentence inscribed as indelibly on the heart of every pre-war regular officer as 'Calais', by her own account, was on Mary Tudor's: 'Time spent on reconnaissance is seldom wasted.' Though it remains by far the best military maxim (its application by no means confined to matters military) in this instance I felt that for the three senior white leaders of the battalion to desert their columns for twenty-four hours in order to carry out such a patrol was stretching it too far. The risk may have been slight, yet risk there was; and without a commensurate object. Any one of our rifle platoon commanders could, in my view, have discovered just as much as three field officers. But I wasn't able to budge Peter, who I think put down my objections to excessive caution if not outright wind-up. Since I made no secret of misgivings, and continued to sulk throughout the patrol, further fuel must have been added to Peter's suspicions.

Guided silently through the forest by a pair of Kachin levies, we spent a night en route concealed in a thicket and next morning crept to the outskirts of Ywathit to survey the village from behind a plantain tree on a mound. We saw no sign of life. Immediately in front of us lay an acre or two of long grass, then clustered thatched roofs and a white pagoda and beyond these, as ever, the enigmatic ranks of jungle trees.

The day after we had returned from this curious expedition Peter flew with Calvert in a light-plane to White City, hoping to pick up information about his battalion's future movements. Back before dark, he brought with him a sack of mail. These letters, parachuted over White City, our original destination, were the first we had received since leaving Assam; that they had dropped like manna from the heavens making them doubly precious. I read every one of mine over and over, forgetting where I was and becoming altogether human again, soft and emotional, moved nearly to tears by the words of a girl who said she had prayed for me in an empty church. Sentiment cleansed us; we felt greatly heartened and sustained. Tomorrow's Ywathit fight seemed no longer paramount.

At about nine next morning, 1st May, I was waiting for the word from Peter to move forward. The rifle platoons of both columns knelt in the grass our side of the plantain tree, Dicky's men to the right, Nobby Hall's X Company to the left; Peter's plan – in the circumstances the only one possible – to advance like beaters through a pheasant covert, the boundary between columns a sandy path dividing the village houses into two groups. Ywathit seemed to lie asleep in the sunlight, the tall pagoda gleaming white above the roofs. The bodies of the waiting, crouching Africans, who had been extended into line, were hidden by the long grass, their bush hats showing like rows of big corks floating idly on a green lake. Listening to the thump of a mortar baseplate being driven home, my eye catching a flash or two from the rifleman's bayonets, I felt exactly the same sort of pitched-up nervous anxiety I had known as a small boy when summoned to the headmaster's study.

After a brief mortar bombardment the Nigerians advanced. 'Direct air support' had been asked for, but no planes arrived overhead and we couldn't afford to wait all day. At the foot of the mound we found a river previously unobserved, slow-running and dark, and waded through it with water to our waists, holding weapons high. On the far side of it appeared first a steep bank and then a belt of undergrowth between canal-like stream and wooder houses. Officers struggled to keep their soldiers in line; like sheep, men tended to follow one another through gaps in the bushes and I found myself having to shout the commands bawled by sergeant-majors on barrack squares. The two mortars ceased to drop bombs when we reached the houses. I cannot recall hearing our Vickers guns, continuous flanking fire from them having been an important feature of Peter's plan. Peering into window spaces and under houses, grenades ready, we saw neither enemy nor inhabitant, the houses themselves mute but bamboo fences, brittle with age, snapping under soldiers' boots like crackers at a party. It began to look as if the Japanese garrison had flitted. We pressed ahead at a smarter pace, clearing the last of the village houses and plunging into the curtain of lantana beyond.

Lantana was a low bush or shrub strongly in evidence near Shan villages. It seemed to be a growth of the valleys – one saw none in the Kachin hills – flourishing in dense thickets, not impenetrable but reducing movement to slow motion; and since it was adhesive rather than prickly its tendrils, or suckers, seized rapaciously upon every part of one's equipment. To attack through lantana, so I had been told, was hair-raising, visibility limited to a yard or two; the Japanese exploited its characteristics to advantage and sited their neat foxholes cleverly. Having come across the stuff often enough, now I met it head on. I could see or feel nothing but lantana tentacles snatching at my limbs; and engulfed by hostile seas of vegetation very quickly lost touch with every single officer and man of my command.

After I had crawled some way a short burst of enemy automatic fire from one flank made me start violently. It must have been a signal. The deep-throated, deliberate clatter of Japanese 'woodpecker' heavy machine guns at once spread rapidly across the undergrowth from left to right, the air crackling, severed leaves fluttering from tree and bush. The sound resembled a bass-voiced, immensely amplified parade-ground *feu-de-joie*. For a moment I hesitated, ears assailed and mind confused, the lantana's embrace surely deliberate, the blind tendrils holding me captive for bullets to strike down. Then, shouting encouragement to my men (wherever they might be) at the top of my voice, I began to creep forward again, hoping to God that the enemy would be shooting a couple of feet too high. The noise of battle was becoming less one-sided. Though failing to suppress the vociferous and busy Japanese machine guns, Brens as well as British rifles and grenades joined in at this stage. When the first fury of the enemy defensive fire spent itself there followed a momentary lull and I could hear soldiers crawling about in the bushes, though whether ours or enemy I had no notion. Intermittent shooting sounded from in front, behind me and on both flanks. The belt of lantana seemed without end.

At last, forcing my way out of the evil bushes and into sunlight, I found myself on the edge of a broad cart track running across what I thought to be the line of our advance. Two Japanese heavy machine guns, one on either flank, now took it in turns to fire more or less continuously down its length from very close range and I dived to the ground. Desperately looking about for cover I spotted a small tree, the only one growing by the cart track on our side, and crawled to it, flattening my body like a lizard. Not a soul was to be seen. I felt overwhelmed by fear, loneliness and self-pity. I wanted a friend's eye to witness what surely must be my end and bellowed to my platoons to get a move on: it had dawned on me that they must be some way behind. The Japanese heard. Every time I opened my mouth one or other machine gun would open fire, chips of wood and bark from the tree-trunk falling on my back or striking me in the face. I was forced to shift my body from one side of the tree to the other according to which gun happened to be in action, the bole, by no means thick, seeming to shrink with every burst to the diameter of a twig.

I don't know how long it can have been before I could see Dicky, Denis Arnold and my staff officer crawling towards me through the lantana, with them a bunch of Nigerians. I shouted to the party to move no further forward. From the cart track the ground sloped gently down to where they gathered, so that they lay in something of a dip, which if it failed to offer much protection against the bullets cracking over their heads was better cover than none. To be pinned down like this ahead of my rifle company struck me as ridiculous, but for the sake of example I decided to remain by my tree rather than crawl back, which in any case I didn't feel very keen to attempt.

Out of nowhere Steve Elvery appeared at my elbow, armed with a rifle. Before I could prevent him he was kneeling on the edge of the track, a yard to my left. Mercifully neither gun opened up.

'Get back, you bloody idiot! You'll be shot!' I said.

'Just a sec sir – having a squint. My God, there's a Jap!'

He put up his rifle and fired.

'Got him. There's another!'

Steve fired again, he might have been shooting rabbits. He had managed to let off a third round before in strong language I ordered him back to his platoon. The three Japs he shot had appeared by the cart track within thirty yards of us, Steve said. He couldn't miss.

As soon as Steve Elvery had gone one of the two machine guns started hammering away and Garaba Gonari was hit. In the hollow now, he must earlier have lost me in the lantana. I heard him tell Dicky in his usual slow voice that he had been wounded, but Dicky's ears failed to catch the uncomplaining words. Fiercely he ordered Garaba to shut up talking and before I could intervene another spray of bullets drowned voices. When the next pause came I told the boy to make his way to the village if he could.

It was pretty clear that we could advance no further without risk of considerable loss, and first we would have to get the Africans to their feet. No supporting fire would be expected even if possible to arrange; we lay too near the Japanese.

Peter Vaughan's voice, high and clear above the sounds of battle, came through my 'walky-talky' radio set, a new acquisiton I had forgotten to use.

'Hello, Charles? How are things going? Where are you?'

I told him where I thought we were.

'We could make a shot at advancing,' I said, 'but I think there'll be a good many casualties if we do.'

'No. Stay put. How did you get that far? 35 are stuck at the north end of the village. I'm by the pagoda.'

Greatly relieved that my dashing Commanding Officer had decided we should attempt no more for the moment, I began to supply him with a more graphic and detailed picture of the situation – mine in particular – until interrupted by the enemy who, hearing a voice, let fly with one of the 'woodpecker' machine guns. This time the Japanese fire made me more angry than fearful. Seizing a Bren from a man behind me, I manoeuvred it round the tree trunk and emptied one magazine in the direction of the Japanese gun on the left and another at tree tops where I suspected snipers might lurk. The Africans behind, much entertained, began to laugh with pleasure and playing up to them I changed weapons, aiming a succession of rifle grenades into a tangle of brushwood fifty yards away on the enemy side of the cart track.

Towards midday Peter, over the hand radio, instructed us to pull out, a step to which I offered no objection. Shouting in Hausa –

Japanese sometimes understood simple military commands in English – I ordered all platoons to make their way back to the pagoda, where Peter had his headquarters.

Deciding to cover my men's withdrawal, for which task I found myself ideally placed, I commandeered Sergeant Umoru Numan, who lay close by, to act as willing accomplice. Setting ourselves up as a two-man rearguard we loosed off with Bren guns into the jungle ahead and on either flank in the hope of persuading the Japanese that they were still threatened. Perhaps deceived, they made no attempt to leave foxholes and launch the standard counter-attack, for which we ought to have thanked our stars. Though I didn't fully realise it until later, Umoru and I would have stood no sort of chance. We exchanged nervous smiles and a few minutes after everybody else had disappeared let go our last long bursts. I left my tree and crawled away. The lantana tendrils appeared miraculously to have lost powers of adhesion, and brushing them aside without much trouble I wriggled through dark tunnels towards the pagoda, trying to suppress a compulsion to move with undignified speed now that my back had been turned to the enemy. At this point I realised that I had left a precious First War .45 revolver, not mine but borrowed, somewhere near the cart track.

As soon as I felt myself out of the Japanese grasp a tidal wave of wild exhilaration swept over me. I might have been drinking champagne with some new and utterly bewitching girl. All colours were enhanced, they glowed. The pagoda now looked whiter than snow; the pretty brass bells crowning it shone more bravely than when we had crept past them earlier that morning; green leaves glistened like emeralds. My Nigerians, sweating and quiet but by no means downcast, stood by in platoon groups awaiting orders and a quick check showed no leader unaccounted for. I reported to Peter Vaughan (who said he was glad to see me), then we all trooped back through the empty village. Soldiers detailed for the task set fire to the wooden houses as they passed, in order to deny shelter to the enemy, and Ywathit became a mass of crackling flames, black smoke billowing. The Japanese, waking up at last, began wildly to shoot into the smoke and finding myself still carrying a Bren gun I continued as unofficial rearguard, this time with Sergeant Major Kitt, who had a Sten. Turning about, we fired a number of random bursts towards the lantana, reaching the river bank as the last enemy bullets raised spray.

Behind the grassy mound I found both columns ready to move

off. No 35's mortar was being strapped to the back of its mule, which had been hit; the soldiers wiped sweat from their faces with their shirt sleeves and gazed at the busy flames. Lighting a cigarette, I was embarrassed to notice how much my hands shook. The feeling of exhilaration was fast slipping away.

A fight, for an hour or two after it had taken place, was more terrifying in retrospect than in reality. One could see dangers most clearly when they threatened no longer. Therefore every man in the column remained silent when he reached the harbour where we had left packs. In silence the Nigerians made fires and brewed tea, cleaned weapons, dried sweat-soaked clothing, their minds hard to read. After the noise of shooting the jungle struck one at preternaturally quiet, like the calm following a thunderstorm. Later on the grip of reaction loosed its hold and suddenly, spontaneously, the Africans began to talk. More for his own relief than the entertainment of friends every black soldier relived aloud his Ywathit experiences, scarcely listening to his comrades, enlivening chatter with gesticulation and laughter, released from the inhibition imposed by fear. In retrospect their fighting had turned into a kind of light-hearted adventure.

Peter and I also spoke about the raid. Always generous, he gave me credit that I did not deserve.

'And do you know,' he added, 'on that recce to Ywathit I almost thought you were starting to get nervy!'

'I've been nervy, as you call it, the whole bloody time.'

'My dear Charles, what absolute tripe. Look at you today – you did damned well!'

Nobody would better have relished masquerading in the cloak of bold commander if only it had fitted; but landing up in front of all one's men, powerless to exert much influence until they withdrew, couldn't in honesty be described as doing damned well.

Talking to the Africans, I found it impossible to trace any pattern in the Ywathit fighting. Loose ends refused to tie up.

'Momman Zaria, how did you get on? How many "Japans" did you shoot?'

'Lord, so many bullets fled past my head that they could not be counted. And then, there before me, a few feet away, I saw a dozen evil Japans. I called Audu, the Bren gunner, and he slew many. Perhaps there were more than twelve – twenty, perhaps!'

I tried to look stern.

'How many did you see with your own two eyes?'

'Eight, sir – eight at least, I swear by Allah!'

'And you, Bako? What is your story?' I asked another.

'I crawled through the bushes, master, and suddenly a Japan grenade fell close to my feet. Woosh! Off it went. But Allah saved me, and here I am, without a wound!'

Bako smiled broadly.

Beneath a stand of high trees lay a dozen wounded men waiting to leave by pony or stretcher for the light-plane strip at Naman. My orderly, looking bewildered, was one; he had been shot through the shoulder. I tried to cheer him up.

'My pain is but slight, master,' he said, 'and I feel joy in seeing you. It was at first said you had been killed.'

'Not me, Garaba. And as for you, this evening or tomorrow an aeroplane will come to take you west over the hills to a hospital in India, where there are many beds with white sheets. Soon you will be well.'

'Yes, so it has been said. My pack, lord, lies under the tall black tree by the stream. Some of your things are in it; I was carrying them.'

Garaba's sad monkey face troubled me. Like many a wounded African he found it hard to take in what had happened to him and his resignation was a reproach. Poor Garaba was too young, too ignorant of life to have been hurt fighting for a British cause entirely beyond his understanding.

In the cool of the evening we trudged back towards the bivouac at Naman, in the foothills, whence we had marched two days before. As we skirted the Naman strip I noticed the wounded waiting for a plane – a forlorn, isolated group far out on the long green tongue of paddi, the ponies which had carried them standing tethered to a tree by the side of the path, nibbling the marsh grass. It resembled a scene from a Victorian narrative painting.

On the day following the Ywathit encounter Peter received the expected order to leave Calvert's group and bring his battalion to a given rendezvous in the vicinity of White City. We were to join the rest of the Nigerian Brigade. Calvert, visiting our harbour to say farewell and wish us Godspeed, praised our work. A request to retain both columns under his command having been turned down by Force Headquarters in India, he had no option, he told us, but to let us go. The brigadier had nursed us carefully. Notwithstanding our total lack of experience when we had joined him, another commander of men as battle-worn as his would certainly have pushed us further in order to spare as far as he might his own brigade. This was the last we saw in Burma of that rugged face and formidable frame, Peter as grieved as myself to part with so notable a leader.

# CHAPTER 13

# North to Indawgyi Lake

An interlude near White City marked the end of the first phase of our modest contribution to the Chindit campaign. It was the second week in May; we had been in Burma a month, had served out our apprenticeship. The days' routine events – patrols and sentries, the loading, unloading and care of mules and ponies, evening and dawn bivouac drills, the sifting and collation of demands for air supply or replacements, the organisation of the drops themselves, all the various tasks were carried out smoothly and as a matter of course. Every officer and man, having learnt his part in the play, also understood the interwoven plot. And like savages at war with a neighbouring tribe we cultivated silence, stealth and continual vigilance.

Ready to believe that years rather than a bare month separated me from a softer, gentler world, I found it impossible to recapture the vanished essence of *douceur de la vie* except in dreams. Nothing but physical comforts of the most basic description gave sensuous pleasure now: hot tea and coffee, eating, smoking, halts on the march, the wonderful feeling of lightness and ease when one's pack would be dumped at the end of the day's tramp. A tired soldier – and we were always tired – could sleep as soundly on damp earth under a tree as in a four-poster with sheets and a mattress. If white men in the column should show themselves quicker to grumble about their surroundings than accept them, the black riflemen, accustomed to living simply and demanding little, adapted easily and without complaint. Making no effort to fight the jungle, they surrendered to it.

While all fighting men on active service must expect to undergo periods of sharp nervous tension, for us there could be little respite from it. There was no question of looking at the map and pointing to a marked line separating Japanese on one side of it from Chindits on the other; unless physically held by Japanese or British, every acre remained Tom Tiddler's ground. No Chindit soldier could at any time consider himself secure from enemy ambush or night attack, however miniscule the possibility; nor could he hope for periods of rest and recuperation behind the front. No front existed. It became a joke that one might meet Japanese round the next corner, but it was literal truth; and when one corner had been negotiated another appeared just ahead.

Nervous strain was to prey upon us always, but most fiercely when we suffered much from hunger, extreme physical fatigue or both, at which times it afflicted us in the form of an exaggerated apprehension of danger real or imagined. More commonly, stress manifested itself as a constant, nagging sense of unease, varying in degree, for which neither palliative nor cure could be offered. We seldom allowed our anxiety to show on the surface. We did our best to hide it, as a man will try to banish from his mind a memory of which he feels ashamed.

The African troops, unlike their white leaders, possessed an enviable faculty for blotting out or ignoring past and future terrors and living entirely in the present. They weren't at the moment being threatened, were they? Well then, why worry!

Though the battalion rested no more than a mile north of White City, I myself had no occasion to revisit the block. In these last days of the dry season the paddi looked browner than it had, but the glider's broken wing, just visible from our harbour, still pointed skyward as though reproaching the heavens for its destruction. Since I had slept by it with Nobby Hall, Steve and the rest of the advanced party on that unforgettable first night the weathered fuselage, so I heard, had acquired some shot-holes, Japanese snipers having found it useful cover. No attack worthy of the name had been mounted against the block since Calvert's second preventive effort, but Mawlu was back in enemy hands. Unknown to us, though the White City garrison must have suspected it, more Japanese soldiers haunted the vicinity, preparing for an all-out assault, than there had ever been. As forewarning of enemy intentions we had seen on the very day we reached the railway valley two dozen Japanese fighters circling and diving, bombing and machine-gunning the scarred hills.

Peter dispatched small ambush parties to several local tracks and was disappointed when they caught nothing. Such minor warlike activities apart, we did little for four days or five except to eat rice, dried potatoes, British 'meat and vegetable' rations and other sybaritic fare dropped over White City. During this interlude, looking to White City for shield, white leaders felt free to pay calls, eat with and chat to one another, laugh and joke in company. Several of us occupied ourselves with composing, or making a shot at composing, satirical and libellous verses to familiar soldiers' airs, many aimed at General 'Vinegar Joe' Stilwell, the American overall commander of operations in Northern Burma of whose baneful influence, sensed rather than documented, we were slowly becoming conscious; but libel laws apart I'm afraid that the mildest of these effusions would do little to enhance the tone of this narrataive if committed to print.

This pause in operations was an exception to the rule, imposed throughout our Burma travels, that the 400-odd soldiers in the column must remain quiet men, noise of any kind to be discouraged. My daily evening orders to assembled senior commanders gave opportunity for them briefly to meet, but in general there could be little other than casual contact between officers, or between British NCOs, with differing responsibilities. A junior white leader, marching, eating and sleeping close to his Nigerian soldiers day after day, was never off duty, social visits to particular friends therefore sadly infrequent. In spite of this there existed a striking, an almost tangible unanimity of spirit which made me proud. Surrendering to some extent his own volition, every individual became absorbed into a column consciousness or identity.

Peter and I found it ominous that dysentery, malaria and other diseases and disabilities should have claimed a toll so early. For three weeks the sick, trailing along with their columns, had given place in the light-planes to the wounded, but as by now a number had become too ill to march further Peter took advantage of the White City air strip and made arrangements to have them flown to Indian hospitals. However reluctant to leave their friends, sick men imposed a burden on us and they had to go.

Though I lost three British NCOs from No 29 Column, the man most regretted by me was Adamu Hadeijia, Steve Elvery's Muslim sergeant, who could barely walk, let alone demonstrate the qualities I felt sure he possessed. Of the rest Dicky Lambert, gaunt and white and attacked persistently by diarrhoea, looked in poor shape and Kitt worse. The blond Sergeant Speak, who had done well, had feet mysteriously swollen and was finding it an effort to keep up. Losses from both columns were made good. Replacements joined us: not, strictly speaking, reinforcements but men of our own, those left behind when bad weather had temporarily closed Lalaghat airfield after Peter had flown in with the bulk of the battalion. Marching from Aberdeen later on, they had been attached to the 12th Nigeria at White City, our men chancing to suffer more than proportionately heavy loss, several being killed and two of the five original officers of Nobby Hall's X Company very seriously wounded. Nonetheless we left the railway corridor stronger in numbers than on the first day of operations.

Brigadier Gillmore's health collapsed and he was flown out, his successor as commander of the Nigerians a brigadier called Ricketts, a fellow light infantryman, without previous experience of African troops. He ruled at White City.

Chris Harrison, now brigade-major to Ricketts, visited our harbour when he could spare the time and we would swap news. Chris's hair was dark but a young and surprisingly red beard dramatically altered the contours of his face. We British looked more like stage pirates every day, most of us cultivating beards still sprouting then but later on, in some instances, to achieve Old Testament grandeur and dignity, mine in the grower's opinion among the finest.

One morning I sent Captain Fisher to buy if he could a water buffalo for the Africans, who relished fresh meat and got none. Instead he returned with a Kachin village headman from the nearer hills, an old man with a creased yellow face like half-cured leather.

'He wants to know whether the White City garrison intends to remain in the valley,' said Fisher.

The block was to be abandoned in forty-eight hours' time; but I had explicit instructions that on no account was this news to reach the ears of Kachin or Shan.

'Tell him the British and their allies are staying until the Japanese are driven away,' I replied. I had no choice.

The old fellow, making a gesture of acknowledgement, began to talk, indeed to embark on something of a speech.

'He says he is glad to hear this,' reported Fisher. 'Japanese sent for him yesterday morning but he wouldn't go. He doesn't think they'll come for him as long as we remain, he says, but they suspect he's been giving us information. He's an old man now, he says, too old to move his family deeper into the hills for safety. He wishes us good luck.'

By far the greater number of the hill-dwelling Kachins, unlike Shans of the valleys, whose allegiance remained suspect, hated the Japanese and killed them when they could. Loyal to the British power, they often risked their lives to assist us, but even among Kachins there might be one or two who would give us away for opium or thirty pieces of silver. An attack on White City during the night fixed for its evacuation could well have proved disastrous.

The headman bowed and took his leave. Convinced he would

accept without question my lie, it was with feelings of shocking guilt that I watched him walk away. The British, the friends he looked to, had for their own reasons been forced shamefully to betray him.

At sunset a couple of days later we girthed and loaded mules, slung packs against wincing shoulders and moved from wooded shelter west across the paddi to establish ourselves on two lonely hills rising like islands from a darkening sea. It was planned to empty White City of its stores and equipment in one night, our job to defend the Dakota strip against threat from the north. From dusk onward aircraft, landing and taking off, continually roared overhead, their silhouettes putting out the stars. The Japanese, watching from Mawlu, must have imagined battalion after fresh battalion being flown in to reinforce the defences; caught off balance, they made no attempt to intervene and to their great credit Brigadier Ricketts, Chris and everybody else concerned in it carried out the secret, meticulously planned evacuation without hitch, by dawn scarcely a man or weapon remaining on that stinking but honourable battlefield.

In a long, silent line we shuffled further west the following morning, splashing through the stream my superfluous advanced party had crossed on its way from White City to rejoin the battalion more than a month before, and after a heavy, sweaty trudge through the soft sand of a dry river bed found a suitable spot for our night harbour.

With the other two battalions of the Nigerian Brigade, the 6th and 12th, we were to tramp north through the Kachin Hills by jungle trails, this time west of the railway corridor, finally to establish ourselves on the range above Indawgyi Lake. This lake, a fat blue caterpillar on the map, lay eighty miles away. An all-British Chindit brigade, 14, headed in the same direction, our joint mission to safeguard the establishment of a new large-scale road and railway block code-named Blackpool to be set up by 111* Chindit Brigade near Hopin. The route, every inch of it, took us up and down steep forest hills, as usual against the grain of the land, if any existed. Eighty miles measured on the map would be many more for marching men on the ground, and daily the monsoon rains were expected.

At first, following paths through gently sloping teak forest, we

---

\* Though brigades and columns were designated by numbers, these bore no relation to the actual number of Chindit formations on the ground.

made satisfactory progress, though the air felt heavier now and we heard distant rumblings of thunder. Between teak trees which had shed most of their foliage the sun struck malevolently down, the powdery dust from dead leaves underfoot irritating throats and making us very thirsty; but water, soon all too plentiful, became difficult to locate. Of the hundreds of little streams shown on the map one couldn't tell without inspection which at that season held water and which did not. Occasionally we were driven to dig deep into the sand of dried-up river beds.

'We can't drink that stuff, sir, surely?' said Steve Elvery.

'Why not? It's wet.'

'But won't it be salty? And what about the bugs in it, sir! I'd rather die of thirst, honestly.'

'It's been filtered through the sand. The Kerens say it's perfectly OK and they should know. Anyway we're going to drink it. You and the mules.'

'Oh. Well if the Kerens say so I suppose it's all right. I've decided not to die of thirst after all. I'd be hard to replace, wouldn't I, sir?'

'If we get no replacements you would!'

After painfully thirsty days, my column found itself lining the edge of a cliff looking down on the confluence of two little rivers a hundred feet below. Like Cortes' men we stared at each other: his cannot have been more surprised than mine to see water, and ours was fresh. Where the rivers met rose an islet, an extravagance of bushes, creepers and grasses looking brilliantly green against the sombre forest. Between banks and islet the water ran glass-clear over a gravel bed; one could distinguish every thread of waving weed, every pebble and small poised fish. Tiredness and worry alike were thrown off with our filthy uniforms and all of us, black and white, plunged in, surrendering to the water's clean embrace, splashing about and laughing like children in Arcadia, life precious.

Before we had marched another half dozen miles clouds began ominously to gather, thunder bellowed and the jungle held its breath. After minutes of tension the monsoon rain, a grey, moving wall, swept over the hills. In less than half an hour the steep single-file track we followed, changing first into a rushing rivulet and then into a sticky ooze of thick brown mud, was rendered next to impassable for every soldier except those in the vanguard of what we called the 'column snake'. The boots and hooves of the leading group and

their animals had trampled it into a morass and one after another
the mules halfway down the column and further back began to fall,
as though pushed to the ground by the hand of some sportive giant.
Lying on their sides and rolling their eyes, pinned to the mud by the
weight of their loads, mules struggled and kicked out frantically as
they strove to regain a foothold. Every load had to be unstrapped
and taken up the hill on the heads of Africans: wireless sets and batteries, mortars and their bombs, machine guns, chests of silver
rupees; while officers and sergeants, slithering up and down the
track, exhorted their men and gave help where needed. Unhappily
we discovered our webbing equipment to be by no means waterproof. Rain was absorbed by and penetrated packs, haversacks and
pouches, adding so greatly to their weight that we staggered under
them. Hoarded food was ruined, cherished letters from home
became shreds of sodden paper. All day we struggled, but when
night came and skies momentarily cleared had been able to climb
no higher than five hundred feet.

From that day on the monsoon played a major role in our lives.
The kind of scene described was to be repeated times without number, becoming routine, an element of practically every day's
march, hardly a matter for comment other than curses. To say that
rain never ceased would be to exaggerate. Five hours of it might be
followed by a spell of hot sunshine before once again the skies
turned black. But rain fell much more frequently than the sun
shone, its volume imperceptibly increasing until by July there
would be rainstorms for five or six successive days with scarcely a
break between them. After that, and as gradually, it diminished. In
August the sky might remain blue for two days together and rain be
gentler when compared with the steady, violent downpour of the
monsoon's height.

We coped as best we could. The Africans, learning from Fisher's
native Kerens, cobbled together rough beds from bamboo and
slept a foot above the ground, arranging groundsheets tied together
with parachute cord over their heads. The British in the battalion,
better off, had dropped to them at this stage excellent American
jungle hammocks having waterproof roofs and bottoms with sides
made of strong mosquito netting, the whole thing in one piece, and
light. The sides opened and closed with a zip fastener. Invidious they
may have been, but none of us proved strong-minded enough to
refuse one.

We learnt how to light fires with wet tinder and became expert at cutting steps and traverses on the muddy flanks of hills; while from careful study of the lie of the land one could hope to select bivouac areas the least likely to be soaking. We also expended great ingenuity in efforts to keep dry, or dry enough, our spare clothing and personal possessions. An immediate consequence of the monsoon was the uncertainty of supply drops, which from now on had to take place in daylight. Even then, rain or blankets of low cloud would be apt to hide the best-laid of signal fires from a Dakota pilots' searching eye or foul weather to prohibit flying altogether.

From the march to Indawgwi Lake to the end of our operations the monsoon proved to be a more consistent and relentless enemy than the Japanese. When downpours continued unabated one couldn't but lose the battle; breaking through every defence, rain mutilated sleep and made life miserable beyond telling

On the way to the lake, and for a long period thereafter, Brigadier Ricketts and his modest retinue formed part of one or other of our battalion columns and fell in with our routine, the Nigerian Brigade Headquarters being inadequately staffed with black soldiers and incapable of protecting itself as a separate entity. Abdy Ricketts, soldierly-looking, dark-haired and with a clipped moustache, a courteous man and eager commander, quite fearless, neither breathed down my neck nor interfered in any way with the running of my column. But he observed closely everything that went on, having selected our battalion to march with, I imagine, because of his three it happened to be the only one mobile from the start, never cooped up in block or 'stronghold'. In military jargon, we 'knew the form'. Our brigadier might occasionally offer advice or suggestion, and should a mule tumble over a hillside or other accident delay us would lend a hand like everybody else, never losing his temper. The rest of us did so several times daily.

The Kachin hills, a few thousand feet high, we found endless, slippery and sheer, on their summits villages with unpronounceable names perching precariously, the country at large wild, forbidding and beautiful, the all-pervading jungle dense. When the storm clouds chose to retreat the sun at first would peer wanly, like a sick man, then gradually gain in strength and warmth from moment to moment as the sky changed from colourless to bright blue. Steam like mist would rise from the forest leaves, from the coats of the mules, our clothing; the torrents lately cascading down the slopes would sink into the ground and the air be filled with the fragrant smell of damp earth and vegetation. Our soaked jungle-green uniforms would quickly dry and at halts on the march every man except the sentries would lie spread-eagled in the generous sunshine, selecting spots where the jungle canopy allowed its stippled shafts to caress and warm him.

Idi Melor, orderly in place of poor wounded Garaba, used to wake me an hour before dawn but never fail to bring tea at least five minutes after every other man in the column was drinking his. It was maddening.

'In the name of Allah, Idi, why are you late yet again?'

'The wood and dead leaves are exceedingly wet, lord. It is difficult to make fires in this evil land where it rains always!'

'How then was it that all the others make fires hours ago?'

At this Idi would grin, his eyes turning up at the corners, an indulgent yet satirical expression appearing on his face. We exchanged the same remarks every morning and evening and I knew quite well what he would say next.

'Sir, my stomach is sick, truly it is. There are many snakes inside me and they crawl about, round and round. They cause much pain!'

His lazy smile would become a devilish kind of chuckle. It was as though Idi hugged to himself some diverting and shocking secret.

After we had swallowed our mugs of tea or coffee at dawn and at the routine midday halt every little cooking fire would be stamped out and scattered, mules be girthed and saddled by their muleteers and loaded by the soldiers who marched with them, pieces of paper and cardboard from ration packets – every scrap – diligently collected and buried. Each man would examine his equipment, meticulously re-arranging the contents of his monstrous pack lest anything badly stowed should chafe backs or shoulder muscles. Then he would heave it up, put his arms through the webbing pack-straps and feel the familiar, sickening wrench as the weight fell against his shoulders and bowed him down.

No sick could be evacuated. We were tramping far from paddi fields, the levelling of light-plane strips out of the question. The monsoon rains encouraged malarial mosquitoes at a period when repeated soakings, night chill and shortage of food had already lowered resistance and for a week the fever-stricken would feel wretched, though marching seemed if anything to mend milder cases. But Kitt and Speak both grew worse and worse, even without packs the hills agony for them as from day to day they struggled on, faces chalk-white and pitifully sunken. They had no choice. Our ponies had enough to do to shift for themselves. Dicky too failed to improve; I felt he couldn't last much longer. We had no wounded with us and came across no Japanese, though a British column in 14 Brigade met with minor disaster when suddenly attacked one night in bivouac. Abdy Ricketts, desperate to take action that might help 111 Brigade at Blackpool, urged his columns onward as fast as they could travel, which could be at no better than a snail's pace. Five miles up and down the sodden gradients represented a good day's march.

Sometimes the two battalion columns shared the same route, on other days paths diverging. When one followed the other, nose to tail, two miles stretched between the van of the first and rear of the second; invariably we moved in single file, no room on the wet, twilit jungle trails for men abreast.

It happens that I possess a few of the pencil-scribbled notes I sent to Peter Vaughan during this march to Indawgyi Lake. By chance he kept them, returning them to me long afterwards; by chance too they survived the rain. These hasty and informal notes refer to none but minor and forgotten incidents, but because written on the spot and unedited they may help to flavour the dish:

Peter. Have received Brigade order and consider it nonsense, as I've no doubt you do. Apart from supply drop question (a) why move from here at 0515 hours to get to a place with *no* water at 0800 hours – that place being only *two miles away?* (b) If no supply drop, suggest we leave at 0630 hours, having fed and watered. How Brigade reckon it will take *3 hours* to get there I can't make out!

Clearly that one was scribbled before the rains. Here is part of another:

To Col. Vaughan: Got caught at 0900 hours by rain. Couldn't get mules (over 20 here) up that first long hill. Three fell over precipice. All loads had to be head-loaded up – long job. New path had to be cut with matchets as old one imposs. through rain. Have stopped for a close-up and brew-up because Europs and Africans absolutely finished and unable to do anything but straggle. Mules OK, one horse fallen with exhaustion but now up again. Will be difficult to carry on if it's a long way, but not

imposs. Am I to (a) bivvy [bivouac] here? (b) Go on up? Present
position: tail just clear of village.

And a third, evidently written when the brigadier was with No
29 Column:

Brigade Commander would like you to send Recce [recon-
naissance] Platoon at 0500 hours to recce bivvy areas in vicinity
LABYA and you to move not after 0630 hours. Can't find Chris so
am writing this for him. Expect you agree that we might push on?
Looks fairly easy going. P.S. Thought it very cunning the way you
oozed past us this a.m. into village! But it was your turn.

Each column divided into four or five permanent 'groups' for purposes of command and emergency defence, the order of march
changed daily, the leading group of one day becoming tail group on
the next and those in-between moving up a place. Thus no group
would be stuck forever at the rear. It was the worst, the most hated
position, since however slowly the leaders walked the pace always
progressively increased down the column snake until the unfortunates at the rear would be killing themselves to keep up, a
phenomenon which may be observed even in a school crocodile of
thirty little boys or girls out for an afternoon walk. As column commander I and immediate staff tramped along near the front, a
privileged place. Should I find myself marching immediately
behind a mule, by the end of that day I would be as familiar with
every contour and blemish, every colour gradation and almost
every hair on its hindquarters as with the outline map of England,
able to recognise many a column animal by one glance at its
backside.

   John MacFarlane, my intelligence officer, acted as No 29
Column navigator. Man-made features, except for tracks and little
Kachin villages connected by narrow forest paths and six or eight
miles apart, didn't exist. Sometimes villages might change location
or altogether vanish; compass and the brown, ominously closely-
spaced contour lines printed on the half-inch maps we carried
remained the only reliable guides to orientation. Interpreting these
lines, comparing them with the little that could be made out
through the overlying forest of the physical features of the country –
spurs and re-entrants, summits and streams – combined with an
accurate judgment of distances tramped (so painfully and slowly),
required great skill. During halts officers would automatically con-

Two of the lorries ambushed by No 29 Column; between them is Denis Arnold. (One of the vehicles seems to have been moved. All were closer together when ambushed.)

A No 29 Column two-man 'scrape' on the ambush position south of White City.

Brigadier Abdy Ricketts pointing out something to John MacFarlane on Hill 60. By John is his orderly, behind him an unknown officer or NCO.

A light-plane over hill forest in Northern Burma. This picture gives a good idea of the sort of country Chindit columns had to traverse.

sult their maps; if John were dubious, ideas of our whereabouts would be pooled. Such a consensus was seldom far out.

Indawgyi Lake became more and more the focal point of our endeavours, a beacon, a promised land beckoning to us from afar. We reached it on a rare sunny morning after fighting our way for an hour through the rank-smelling slime of a swamp in which tall, languidly waving reeds grew high over our heads and reduced vision to zero. Quite suddenly the reeds thinned, the track twisted to the right and I saw ahead an immense and dazzling silver sheet. Every African grinned and pointed, quickening his pace; the one day's rest, a carrot held in front of our noses for a week, looked within easy grasp.

A road of sorts led us to the lake-side village of Nammun. Along its length stood a line of ancient grey telegraph poles I couldn't remove my eyes from. In their homely way they seemed to represent civilization: something forgotten, lost, remote. The rotting poles, their twisted wires lying on the grass in rusting hoops, made a kind of symbolic bridge between past and present.

Nammun turned out to be a large village in which a few Shans lingered. Many of the houses stood empty, including new ones built under Japanese orders and used as barracks. Bomb craters, green with springing new grass, pitted the earth, an uprooted tree sprawling clumsily across the roof of what looked to have been the Japanese Headquarters. To the north a bright green carpet spread to the lake; to the east a range of high hills, steeply rising, towered above houses, marsh and wide expanse of blue-grey water.

Peter, ahead of us, had already sent one platoon from No 35, soon to be followed by others, post-haste to reinforce Geoffrey Lockett's Leicestershire Column, currently holding the Kyunsalai pass through the tall hills. It had been a race between Chindits and Japanese to get there first : no sooner had Lockett seized it than the Japanese attacked him with vigour. It turned the key to the Hopin road, the Japanese anxious to hold it as flank protection for their intended assault on Blackpool, the new block in the railway corridor. Three Chindit brigades had been ordered by General Lentaigne – he who had succeeded Wingate as force commander – to assist Blackpool, or at the very least to show some sort of presence or threat. All failed because of the monsoon: Calvert, still in the hills east of the railway, cut off completely from 111 Brigade at Blackpool by the flooded valley between; 14 Brigade and our own fatally delayed by the rain which had slowed us to a crawl.

My column occupied empty houses in Nammun. It began to pour. Under a roof for once, listening with only half an ear to the faint thud of mortar bombs from the Kyunsalai pass, I felt selfishly glad to be safe and dry. Fisher returned from a foraging expedition with rice enough for everyone – paid for in coin, not appropriated – and after kindling fires under the eaves we drank tea, greedily watching the rice simmer in our mess tins but feeling it a pity that we had no salt. As usual we were overdue for a drop. Fortified by the meal, I began to listen more attentively to the muffled sounds of distant battle and wondered how soon No 29 Column would be drawn in. My men were sheltered and fed, dry and warm; many of Peter's, lying high amongst the rainclouds and without rest or comfort of any kind, under fire. Now that I had a full stomach I felt a twinge or two of irrational guilt.

Several British columns of 14 Brigade marched into Nammun the next day, some tramping off to nearby hills, others resting in the village. Tired, dirty and ragged though all looked, the white soldiers had that unmistakable air of stoical resolve which Chindits seemed to carry like a flag.

Waiting about, half-ashamed of doing nothing, I expected at any moment to receive orders from the brigadier direct, or from Peter, to relieve No 35 Column's men up in the pass, but the sun had set before I was summoned to Brigade Headquarters, to find Ricketts and Chris Harrison ensconced in a tidy house boasting an unsteady table.

Our brigadier, caressing as usual his burgeoning beard, was making characteristic, mysterious-looking passes over a spread-out map, ritual gestures never failing to make me smile. One expected the map to stand up on end and dance a jig.

'We're off tomorrow,' he said, 'we can edge our way' – making the appropriate movement with one hand – 'along the north side of the lake and creep up the hills at this point just here' – his forefinger rapidly circling a square mile or two of contour line – 'and then we'll emerge from Wabaw into open country!' His last flourish, indescribable, indicated triumphant emergence. Catching Chris's eye, I tried to keep a straight face.

Before we left Nammun I put Kitt, Speak and half a dozen Africans into the hands of a doctor in a British column, subsequently hearing from Kitt that he had waited there a fortnight – efforts to build an air-strip on those marshy flats having been abandoned as hopeless – until in the end two Sunderland flying boats had swung

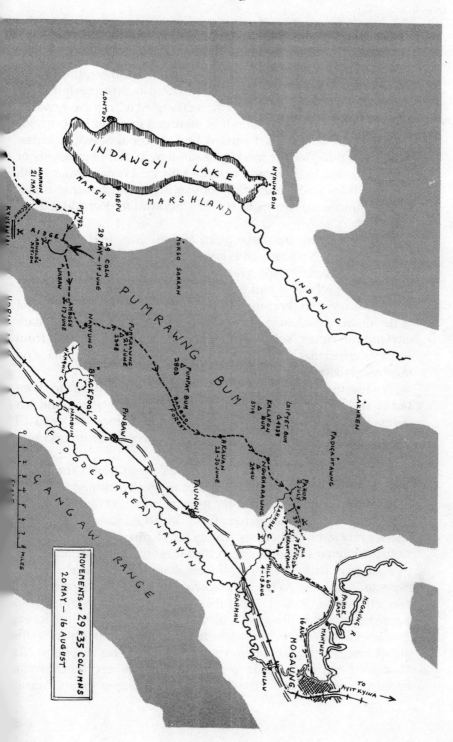

MOVEMENTS OF 29 & 35 COLUMNS
20 MAY — 16 AUGUST

over the hills to splash down like monstrous swans on Indawgyi
Lake and fly away with the accumulating casualties of two brigades.
The flying boats made several journeys, one bringing us as a most
welcome gift Ivor Ramsay, a regular major badly wounded by a
practice grenade at Ibadan and left behind in Nigeria. It was his
revolver I had lost at Ywathit. How he wangled it I can't remember;
none of us had any idea Ram had managed to reach India or, for
that matter, ever would. I missed both Kitt and Speak, Kitt particularly. If not quite the model of a modern British sergeant-major
(slightly to misquote Gilbert-without-Sullivan) his staunchness, soft
Cornish voice and wonderfully pessimistic prognostications had
become intrinsic features of No 29 Column life. Kitt was a good
man.

That evening my troops bivouacked with Brigade Headquarters
five miles from Nammun in evergreen forest at the foot of the formidable Kyunsalai range. Water dripped steadily from every tree
and creeper; all day it had poured. We had waded across a river,
water to our chests, keeping our feet only with difficulty. I thought
of the shelter forsaken in Nammun, the roaring fires, the rice, half-
envying the brave Nobby Hall when we heard by wireless from
Peter Vaughan that he had been wounded by a Japanese grenade on
the Kyunsalai pass and was to be evacuated.

At dawn the column, with Brigade Headquarters, began to clamber up the fiercest gradient we had yet attempted, two thousand feet
in less than a mile. Nothing other than an ill-defined track existed
and the jungle leant perilously over us, the boots of the man climbing in front of me level with my bush hat.

Two elephants cleared the path for us! Their oozies (mahouts)
cut head-high passage with dhars, yelping shrill commands to their
charges the while. The beasts, moving with slow deliberation,
would swing their hindquarters from side to side as delicately they
tested every foothold before planting ponderous feet firmly into the
mud. The oozies straddled their necks, every time its rider elected
to slash at impeding bamboo the elephant waiting patiently until
the man had finished before gingerly exploring its next step. The
two animals had joined our ranks only the previous evening. It so
happened that the (British) Burma Intelligence Corps staff officer at
Brigade Headquarters had been employed by a timber firm in this
area before the Japanese invasion: these were his elephants. At
Nammun, having learnt from friendly Shans whereabouts in the
forest the oozies with their elephants were hiding themselves to

avoid capture by Japanese, he had been able to get hold of them and here they were – master, men and beasts romantically reunited.

Our mules hated the elephants, their very smell anathema; the Africans regarded the animals with doubt and suspicion mixed. In Nigeria wild elephants have nearly disappeared and no soldier could have heard of elephants being tamed. Harnessed and mounted, the huge creatures were an assault upon their credulity.

After a terrible climb we achieved the spine of the ridge, or hog's back, running along the summit of the Kyunsalai range, and after skidding rapidly down the eastern slope exchanged a shot or two with a Japanese patrol, by which time we had been joined by Peter's column, now released from the pass. We tried to get some sleep. The brigadier had given warning of his intention to attack Wabaw, an enemy-held village a mile away on the margin of open country, early the following morning. That night rain simply pelted down; we became saturated and felt wretched. At the thought of rising before dawn, soaking from head to toe and shivering with cold, to issue operation orders to my column and in general act the part demanded of a leader, my spirits began to sink into a bottomless quagmire. In the small hours a cloudburst flattened every African shelter and a stream close to our bivouac area, bursting its banks, engulfed a section of sleeping men. Five rifles and packs were swept away but no man drowned.

After a miserably wet and sleepless night I was attempting in the darkness to gather together wits and nerve when a wireless signal instructed Ricketts to retrace his steps (perhaps because Blackpool, unsupported, had already fallen to the Japanese; but I may have my dates wrong). Looked at objectively, our brigadier's had been a promising move, no doubt the enemy unaware of the path that without aid from the elephants we could never have climbed. Once we had cleared Wabaw of enemy, Abdy Ricketts would have been well placed to aid Blackpool by positive action. But these are afterthoughts: I cannot pretend to have shed a single crocodile tear when the attack was called off. Dropping off a platoon, Blossom's I believe, to counter threats to our rear the battalion, with Brigade Headquarters, turned about and in cascades of rain literally crawled back up the slope on hands and knees to bivouac as best it might on the spine. On the third day, soaked to the skin, plastered with mud and wholly despondent, we found ourselves back where we had started from three days before, which was the foot of the western slopes five miles from Nammun.

On the fourth day Ricketts ordered me up to the top again with Z Company. The spirit of the Grand Old Duke of York must have been hovering overhead.

CHAPTER 14

# A Long Pause and a Weary Trek

Having set up a small tactical headquarters, with John MacFarlane acting as staff officer, I was to remain on the spine of the switchback ridge until about the middle of June. Z Company rifle platoons lay north, south and east, none closer than a mile from my head-quarters and all widely separated. Every week dispositions would be changed as dictated by current intelligence or orders from Brigade; occasionally there might be a game of general post, all pla-toons swapping localities. Two thousand feet below me the remain-der of No 29 Column, all of No 35 and also Brigade Headquarters lived in the jungle at the foot of the Nammun side of the ridge, their address, according to the map, 'Pt 792'. Though a radio set, its long antenna waving, became my telephone to Pt 792, the only certain means of contact with my rifle platoons was by African runner. Walky-talky sets proved unreliable at over a mile. Every day I would write orders (should any be necessary), intelligence information and plain chat on pages torn from my notebook, wrapping them in cellophane from K ration packets to keep them dry and despatch-ing them by runner to Blossom, Steve and Denis. By this means touch could be maintained, the daily newsletter, I hoped, some-thing for the young officers to look forward to. They must often have felt bored, lonely and nervous.

From the top of the ridge everything at a lower level than our cloud-eyrie usually remained invisible, mist drifting about the treetops and floating in hollows where bamboo flourished; but at rare intervals the sun might chase the clouds out of sight and far below us we could see the face of Indawgyi Lake, its green margins freckled with little brown houses. When supplies were being dropped over Nammun on sunny days, we would look down to watch Dakotas whirring round and round like cockchafers on June evenings, their distorted shadows racing behind or ahead of them over the marshes, parachutes falling from them like white petals from a rose and ant-sized figures of soldiers running to collect them.

In spite of frequent rain we kept reasonably dry, opportunity now for the Nigerians to construct bamboo beds more elaborate than those knocked up before dark at the one-night bivouacs punctuating marching days. Really heavy storms, however, would destroy them and within a minute my unhappy men be drenched. As well as mosquitoes the rain brought leeches. Their distribution in the jungle appeared random, some patches harbouring never a leech while others, to our eyes precisely similar, abounded with the unsavoury little animals. One might observe numbers of leeches on the wet leaves of evergreen bushes bordering tracks, heads and bodies raised up in the shape of question marks as they made ready to attach themselves to any moving object brushing past. The creatures, looking like short lengths of bootlace when their stomachs remained empty, were adept at insinuating themselves between trouser and anklet – even though lace holes – and sometimes decided to attach themselves to our private parts, an impertinence providing welcome entertainment for all but the victim. More commonly they fixed on legs or feet. Unless one happened to see patches of blood, or feel it ooozing, their presence might remain undetected until the leeches had become fully gorged, blown up like miniature sausage balloons. A pinch of salt or lighted cigarette applied to their rear ends would make them drop off; it was when foolish or impatient soldiers tried to dislodge the things by force that their heads remained embedded, to cause nasty jungle sores or ulcers. Unpleasing their habits may have been, but leeches never menaced our welfare.

From this time onward I could no longer even pretend to make head or tail of the master tactical plans in presumed conformity with which our columns marched, counter-marched or – as now – sat immobile. Our future had become densely shrouded in the fog of war. Signals emanating from Force Headquarters in Assam, exhorting us to make final efforts in our fight against the Japanese, the elements or both, promising that shortly we should be enjoying the ease of a tented camp and fresh rations in India, came to be received with increasing cynicism. Gradually it became known that, despite appearances, our operations were controlled not by Chindit Force Headquarters but by the American General Stilwell, whose Chinese advanced at so leisurely a pace from the north. It also became known, through the bush telegraph system, that he disliked both the British and their troops, indeed despised them. Many of us began to think that Stilwell must regard Chindits as expendable (a suspicion subsequently discovered to have been perfectly justified). Wingate, a hard man indeed, aware from his own 1943 experiences of the strain, undernourishment and exhaustion bound to dog its steps however little actual fighting it might become involved in, had intended that no Chindit column should remain in Burma for longer than twelve weeks at a stretch. But Wingate was dead.

Instead of sitting like a spider in the middle of its web, waiting for something important to happen, I ought to have visited my out-lying platoons constantly. Brigade was in touch by wireless and John MacFarlane perfectly capable of handling an emergency dur-ing my temporary absence.

I sat tight for too long, allowed too much scope for the introspec-tive thoughts a soldier on active service should strive to hold at arm's length. As caged birds released from captivity will return to voluntary imprisonment after one or two tentative flights, so did my thoughts, after a glance or two at family and friends, inevitably fly back to Burma. Over and over again I reviewed events since White City, examining every incident in analytical detail, indulging in orgies of self-criticism. The standards I had set for myself in the safety of India had been uncompromising, and I had failed to live up to them. Easily I persuaded myself that such professional skills as I possessed were counteracted by a deficiency of what generals called 'officer-like qualities'. I had been too cautious, had lacked boldness and dash.

Self-castigation, whether justified or not, achieved nothing. Its effect was destructive, breeding a sense of failure which in spite of my depression I felt determined at all costs to keep hidden from those under my command. Soul-searching was an indulgence that could neither resurrect the dead nor bring comfort to the living. Once begun, however, it proved hard to stop, gathering its own momentum like a log rolling down a slope. Physical action of some kind was the obvious antidote. I should have realised it at once and forced myself along dim jungle trails to visit my lonely outposts.

Books – any books – might also have helped distract me. During marching days little opportunity for reading occurred; prepara-tions for the day began before dawn and by the time we had reached our bivouac it would, ideally, be an hour or two before dark and many things to be seen to before the light died. Rain had destroyed most of our literature, not voluminous even before the monsoon; anything adding inessential ounces to the weight of packs would be ruthlessly discarded and heavy items, such as the rare bottle of supply drop rum, shared out on the spot. Pieces of one tattered volume of *Decline and Fall of the Roman Empire* were all we could raise between us

by now. I devoured with gratitude a handful of dog-eared pages
ironically and in measured periods describing the vices, follies and
eccentricities of Nero and Caligula, thinking, without much
originality, what an extraordinary contrast so voluptuous a style of
living made with our own loveless and austere existence in country
that must have been beyond the ken of any Roman emperor.

For a week a tree-trunk near my jungle hammock on the ridge was
decorated with numbers of black and yellow-striped longicorn beetles
of great size, boasting antennae of fully five inches. Why didn't I
gather up a specimen or two? They would hardly have over-
weighted my pack! Within sight no other interesting creatures presented themselves, nor at the time had I will or energy enough to
walk a step in search of any.

Throughout our forest wanderings we saw no large wild animal.
However silent they might imagine themselves, four hundred men
with mules tramping along a track in single file flaunted their presence: no sensible beast would linger to watch us sweating by. Sustained whooping choruses from rival gibbons, resounding at dawn
and dusk, startled us until we grew used to hearing them, but one
caught never a glimpse of the long-armed singers in person. An
African soldier once presented me with a rabbit-sized, woolly
primate with melancholy eyes, perfectly circular, which took up
much of its face; probably a slender loris. Daylight confused the little
beast and I returned it to the trees. Occasionally a terrifying crashing of undergrowth in the night would stop all hearts for fear of
Japanese attack – noises made, it was to be supposed, by elephants
(though I don't recall seeing droppings), wild cattle or sambhur.
Should the column have been momentarily scattered by elephants
or straying mule been threatened by a tiger I believe I might have
welcomed the diversion provided no enemy were near nor
damage done.

Two of the platoons in my charge found themselves close to
enemy positions. At the foot of the eastern slopes lay Steve Elvery's
and Blossom's, under Dicky Lambert's direction; from time to time
they had slight brushes with Japanese from Wabaw, the village
which the battalion had been about to attack towards the end of
May before Ricketts was compelled to retrace his steps.

On the ridge itself a corporal from my small headquarters, patrolling south along the path leading to the Kyunsalai pass, reported
finding a telephone cable, a thin yellow snake lying across the track

a mile or so away. This man happened to be one of the few Southern Nigerians in the ranks, in Ibadan days the armourer's assistant.

'Be Japan line,' he said in pidgin. 'Better we go watch 'um. But dem bush bad place too much!'

John MacFarlane volunteered to take one or two Africans, cut the wire and lay an ambush. We regarded the affair as a joke, a kind of treasure hunt. In two hours he came back, producing a Japanese paybook and for treasure a small pocket mirror with a blue tassel.

'A Jap looking for the break came up the hill and almost walked into us. Sule Ankwa shot him through the head but the man hadn't got a weapon, we found. We should've grabbed him.'

I appropriated the mirror, and would sometimes gaze into it to admire my thick black beard and vainly search what remained visible of my features for trace of the refining fires of war.

The next morning I sent Denis Arnold and his platoon to follow the telephone cable towards the pass, telling him to find out first where the receiver might be concealed, and then act as he thought best. Some while after he had gone we heard distant muffled shooting: grenade crumps and a series of bursts from light machine guns which ceased abruptly. Hours passed: John and I began to dread the worst – ambush, annihilation – but just on sunset Denis returned to report. We saw him walking slowly up the muddy gradient leading to our headquarters, obviously very tired, steps deliberate and head bent. When Denis got closer he looked up and broke into a smile of compelling charm. No number of Japanese deaths would have made up for his.

Denis told us that he had followed the yellow line north for a mile before discovering that it led to a knoll, or pimple, halfway between my headquarters and the Kyunsalai pass itself. The pimple overlooked Nammun; everything going on there could have been reported back by telephone to Wabaw when the weather was good enough to observe it. Crawling forward inch by inch, Denis had seen Japanese soldiers sitting about on top. He decided to attack and – remarkably – had got his platoon halfway up the slope before being spotted. He and his men had charged the rest of the way throwing grenades, and after a sharp fight the Japanese, a platoon strong themselves, had fled.

A Japanese platoon of thirty-odd men, always deeply dug-in if allowed half a chance, was never less than a formidable proposition, the more so when holding the advantage of height. It might well take two companies, supported by mortars and machine guns if not aircraft, to overrun it, by which stage the defenders would most of them be dead or incapacitated. For Denis to have attacked without hesitation on his own initiative instead of reporting back to me for orders had been a gallant act. There were, inevitably, some casualties: Denis's orderly, to whom he was greatly attached, had been shot dead.

This feat, which won for Denis an 'immediate' Military Cross, underlined a Japanese tactical weakness: relying upon his very quick reactions our enemy would frequently, arrogantly neglect to post sentries. Consequently he might prove vulnerable to surprise attack, the very thing we on our side strove so hard to avoid. Had the Japanese been properly alert, No 6 Platoon would have stood no chance of success and certainly lost many more men.

After Denis Arnold had returned to his platoon I pondered about the nature of courage. To follow the letter of orders into great danger, even to certain death, requires valour indeed; but true natural courage, having an extra dimension, transcends disciplined obedience. The act is always voluntary and consciously or unconsciously self-sacrificial, whether undertaken on the spur of the moment or deliberately planned. There is a world of difference between this sterner conception and, for example, Lord Cardigan's obedience of a direct order from Lucan to charge Russian guns at Balaclava, for which action he reaped extravagant praise. Cardigan had had no choice but to charge. What if he, his regimental commanders or their troopers had refused to move? There would have been courts martial for cowardice, firing squads at dawn.

The following morning I paid a visit to No 6 Platoon, which had meantime taken over the captured Japanese position as its own. Many friends greeted me, Sergeant Umoru Numan conspicuous. He seemed to enjoy fighting, the Japanese plainly the enemies of his Christian God and of 'Kingi Georgi' both, and whenever he smelt action his agreeable smile would flash like a torch. (As opportunity offered Umoru studied the bible he kept in his haversack, moving his lips as he followed the printed words with a finger.) The private soldiers of Denis Arnold's platoon seemed already to have forgotten they had been in any fight. Living, as ever, for the hour and the day, smoking damp ration cigarettes, overhauling bits of equipment, quietly talking, they looked, I thought, relaxed rather than nervous. The shadow of death had touched them but lightly.

Blossom Eede became the second of Z Company's platoon commanders to be evacuated. Too young for endurance, his big frame had outstripped his stamina and doctor Neil Leitch reported that he must have strained his heart. Certainly poor Blossom looked the shadow of his cheerful self, his vivid red face blotched and streaky, like an actor's when his greasepaint starts to melt. Accidents robbed us also of two African NCOs within a few days of each other. A corporal, examining without due care one of the new American light carbines many officers now carried, stupidly put a bullet through his hand; while Nomman Sokoto, a young sergeant, had the misfortune to strike the butt of his Sten against the ground and shoot himself in the stomach, dying in agony within hours. His death shocked us. That men should be killed in battle had of course to be accepted: to die between actions and by chance cruel indeed.

On 12th June No 35 Column, which since fighting up on the Kyunsalai pass had been resting at Pt 792, with Brigade Headquarters climbed over the ridge and spent the night with Dicky's contingent before breaking a trail towards the railway valley. Leaving my hill-top position to a York and Lancaster column of 14 Brigade, I followed the next morning with the reunited No 29, the long respite from marching making packs feel heavier than ever and leg-muscles no less weary. When we were close to Wabaw, which I skirted somewhat nervously, leaving 'stops' on every track radiating from the village, a storm burst and all traces of Peter's passage were instantly obliterated. Uncertain of his route, I grew worried. We were approaching the long open valley, the enemy garrisons by railway line and road; it struck me as improbable that Peter's march could have gone unnoticed. After struggling for some while through mud, eyeing suspiciously the black, sinister tunnels piercing the trackside undergrowth, we ran into No 35 Column harboured astride one spur of a forested hill rising steeply above the contours of the valley. Peter had already reconnoitred another spur for us, got his men to cut steps across the more treacherous slopes and arranged guides. His forethought warmed me. Without Peter's help we would have floundered about in the slime until after midnight sorting ourselves out.

Ricketts felt satisfied that these jungle-clad hillocks provided an adequately concealed base from which to launch raids against enemy-held villages and supply dumps in the valley.

Z Company had now been taken over by Ivor Ramsay, he who

had arrived by flying boat. Handsome, slight, moustachioed, capable but never obtrusive and with a remarkable gift for satirising to perfection the voices and mannerisms of pompous or stupid generals and their like, Ram's magical reappearance at Nammun after a year's absence from the battalion was bonus indeed. Dicky Lambert now acted as his second-in-command; the two had long been friends and Dicky, a sick man, may have felt relieved to surrender responsibility for the company to the more senior though younger Ram. After announcing that he thought himself better than for weeks, Dicky went on to tell me in his no-nonsense manner that he felt unhappy about the battalion hide-out. So did I. When I surveyed it in daylight prescience whispered that it lacked the security such a base ought to provide. That afternoon two stray Dakotas circled, evidently looking for some other column, but we persuaded them to drop the rations on board to us instead; we needed them. Japanese in the valley may well have observed them doing it.

However that may be, before I had the chance to eat my K ration breakfast the following morning I heard shooting. The noise reverberated, distance and direction impossible to judge. After making sure that none of my own column was involved, I walked the few hundred yards separating us from No 35 and Brigade Headquarters to find out what could have happened. Occasional shots and bangs of grenades continued until I reached Peter's nearest rifle platoon, whose commander knew nothing. At Brigade Headquarters I found Chris Harrison with Peter's column staff officer, Prichard.

'What's going on? What's all the noise about?' I asked.

'I thought you were coming to tell us,' said Chris.

'But surely you've some idea? It's nothing to do with 29.'

'Only that Peter and Llew and about fifteen men left twenty minutes ago on a patrol towards the railway.'

A stray bullet or two whined over the trees; the nearest Africans fingered their rifles, watching us. I was debating whether to stay or return to my column when Peter Vaughan, assisted by an African soldier, stumbled up the path, his face white. Blood seeped through at field dressing untidily clamped to an upper arm; my mind leapt back to the wounded Tich Cooper after the ambush. Peter, always voluble, began to talk so rapidly and in so disjointed a manner that at first none of us could make out what exactly had happened. It emerged that his patrol had been surprised at close range just beyond the supply-dropping ground, a grassy glade a couple of hundred yards away. Mike Llewellyn Davies, who had succeeded the wounded Nobby as X Company Commander in No 35 Column, had been shot dead.

'Alhassan Geiri drove the Japs off with grenades. Alhassan Geiri did damned well. A platoon will fix 'em. Send a platoon along quick!' Peter sat down heavily on an ammunition box while Bob Murray, his column doctor, removed the field dressing and examined the wound. That Mike Llewellyn Davies should have been killed and our colonel wounded in a chance clash seemed incredible, no other man, apparently, having received so much as a scratch. Stupidly I stared at the jagged hole torn in Peter's arm.

Five minutes later I was standing alone in the clearing where yesterday's purloined supply drop had fallen. Beyond it, leading away from the spurs occupied by the battalion, a track ran through jungle along a knife-edged ridge and eventually to the railway corridor. This was the path Peter's patrol had followed. Shocked by Mike's death and Peter's wound, wearing nothing but khaki shorts and a pair of sandshoes, I felt as unwarlike a figure as I must certainly have looked. The brigadier had sent me off posthaste to organise some sort of action against the intruding Japanese: no time to get into jungle green and boots. My orderly Idi Melor having been dispatched with a written message to my nearest platoon, now commanded by a white sergeant, I was impatiently waiting for it.

As the men filed into the open the figures of four African soldiers emerged at the same moment from the jungle at the far side of the clearing, carrying a stretcher improvised from cut bamboo. The platoon halted off the track, waiting for the stretcher bearers to pass by with the body of Mike Llewellyn Davies. It lay peacefully, no wound showing; but as I had feared they would be, my soldiers looked unnerved. Moved more, or perhaps more obviously, by the loss of one of their white leaders than by the deaths of compatriots, perhaps in their hearts the Nigerians believed us less vulnerable than they; perhaps a British death emphasized their own mortality. Miserably they gazed at Llew's calm face, half-hidden by a strong brown beard. They had all known him and almost wrung their hands.

I instructed my sergeant – joined a few moments later by No 35 Column's reconnaissance officer on his own – to patrol for a mile down the track, to anticipate an ambush at any moment, and should it happen to do all he possibly could to assert superiority. It was not a pleasant task to undertake.

For a quarter of an hour I waited in the clearing, listening for shots and half-wishing I had sent Dicky with the patrol. But two senior commanders in one morning as casualties seemed to me enough: The brave and impulsive Peter, once again, had risked himself on a reconnaissance surely not of an importance to warrant the presence of both him and his company commander. At length, unable to bear longer the strain of waiting and now feeling that Ricketts might have wanted me to take personal charge, I followed up my platoon and hadn't walked far along the path before seeing new blood-smears on a tree and a pile of empty Japanese cartridge cases gleaming from the mud. It was the spot where Peter's party had been ambushed.

After five minutes I caught a glimpse of the tail end of the patrol disappearing round a bend in the track. Brushing past half the Indian file of soldiers who, understandably, moved with an exaggerated caution that in other circumstances would have been comical, I was making my way towards the front when I saw the scouts, Peter's officer and one or two other leading men begin to feel their way down a slippery and very steep gradient. Perhaps half a dozen soldiers were over the brow before Japanese opened fire from the green curtain of jungle at the foot of the slope. There followed a wild scramble, all except one soldier safely regaining the crest. The African hit was Garaba Fort Lamy, a man who at Ibadan had endeared himself to me by performing marvellously life-like initations of a jumping frog. He lay spread-eagled on his back astride the path, thirty feet down, groaning like a dying animal until mercifully the next burst of firing finished him. The rest took cover in the bushes either side of the track as a stream of bullets cracked just over their heads.

Hoping by some show of retaliation to put heart into the platoon, I collared a Bren gunner and planted him and his gun on the crown of the slope, but within a few seconds its tattoo ceased, the gunner struck in the face by a Japanese bullet ricocheting off the barrel. Though the Nigerians rallied, bursts of automatic fire greeted us whenever we showed ourselves. We threw grenades down the hill and let fly with Brens from the less dangerous side of the track, but could see nothing of the Japanese party concealed thirty yards away. After a third or fourth African had been hit I decided to break off contact. We had achieved little or nothing – perhaps reacted rather feebly.

Shaken, obviously relieved to escape, the platoon turned about. Mortar bombs – real ones, not the small and comparatively ineffective bombs from enemy grenade dischargers – sped our departure, exploding loud-voiced in the trees. Midway between enemy and supply drop clearing I established the platoon in a suitable ambush position in case the Japanese should decide to come forward and investigate. (They did not. For the Jap patrol leader it had been a better morning's work than he knew; he could afford to rest on his laurels.) Then I walked back to report events to Brigade Headquarters, disappointed, gloomy and very hungry, sweat coursing in rivers down my naked chest.

Since the projected base for raiding operations had become hopelessly compromised, there remained nothing for it but to up sticks. The following morning Ricketts sent me off with No 29 Column to look for a better one, No 35 Column and Brigade Headquarters to follow as soon as food from a second, more complete supply drop, this time ours by right, had been gathered in. Six miles to the north-east we came across a gently swelling hill clothed in rustling bamboo and harboured astride it, some hundreds of feet above a stream running melodiously between sandy beaches. Smoke rose from Namyung, a village a few miles away, reported unoccupied by Japanese; rain hissed and pattered against the bamboo thickets; gibbons whooped. No menace breathed here and no premoniton disturbed Dicky. When No 35 joined us, after collecting the supply drop without too much enemy interference, Brigadier Abdy Ricketts, serene, lavish with gesticulation and still looking for offensive action, bubbled over with fresh raiding plans. He even proposed that his Nigerian Brigade should remain in Burma throughout the monsoon season, a suggestion received with something less than rapture by Peter, Chris and me. We heard no more of it.

Alas for the brigadier's plans! Again they were to be frustrated. A wireless signal from Force Headquarters now instructed him to concentrate his brigade at a Kachin village many miles away. Stilwell was drawing us to the north, further into his net.

If the march from White City to Indawgyi Lake had been exacting, this one called upon all our reserves of fortitude. Light-plane strips were of course as impossible to construct and now we had many more sick, their number increasing daily. No option remained open except to take them with us on foot, on ponies fit enough to carry them and on bamboo stretchers; and we watched in dismay as the battalion snake grew ever more attenuated. Soon after we had left Namyung twenty men lay close to death. The Nammun lakeside huts were, too late, discovered to be infested with the mites carrying scrub typhus, an illness dangerous indeed and without known remedy. Devoted nursing and the will to live were factors which might keep death at bay; and since nursing in the hospital sense of the word was impossible, men died. Acute depression after the worst of the fever had left the sufferer – a common symptom – caused one or two Nigerians actually to commit suicide. Among others Chris Harrison and Denis Arnold collapsed with typhus during this march, both surviving, thank heaven; and Steve Elvery went too, unable to shake off bouts of severe malaria which had, I think, started at Nammun. Almost too weak to walk, Steve joined the straggling procession of sick soldiers.

With no end to our sojourn yet in sight, none but Dicky Lambert and myself of the original nine British of Z Company remained active, and I knew that Dicky, uncomplaining, felt far from well. For every man in the column who had been killed or wounded there were by now a dozen sick, proportionately many more white men than black.

The youngest of the British fared worst; men in their early twenties proved to be sprinters rather than marathon runners. Fresh, they would be capable of considerable exertion, able to march further and more quickly than men rather older, but having had few years in which to build up stamina suffered more from lack of sleep, shelter and food. While these young platoon commanders and white sergeants, burning themselves out, fell ready victims to fever or other ill, mature men from the late twenties up to about thirty-five years old had a good chance of finishing the course if not cut down in action or by typhus: their stamina had reached its peak and hardships bore upon them less heavily. Very few in their forties took part in the Chindit campaign. The unrelenting physical effort wrung from ageing muscles was too much for all but the strongest, though Abdy Ricketts, several years older than any man in our battalion except for Fisher, must have been approaching that age. If he hadn't been in Burma for quite as long as we, he endured both killing marches and to the end showed no obvious diminution of physical or mental force. Our courteous brigadier proved tough and resilient as leather.

Ill with malaria myself for a spell, though not seriously, I sweated and shivered alternately, figurehead rather than commander,

memories of this cruel march remaining fragmentary. Though I
believe I kept it well hidden, the fever's death left me in a pro-
foundly pessimistic state of mind: Burma earth, I thought, would in
the end receive the skeletons of every man of us. 'One last effort'
constantly being demanded by signal, when or where we were supposed to make it we hardly cared, our more immediate concern to
keep moving towards our rendezvous, a distant village called
Pahok. Coming across no Japanese, we felt grateful to be spared a
fight; we needed every particle of energy to put one foot in front of
the other. Few trails led in the right direction and of these several
had become impassable. Twice or three times the battalion was forced
to hack a way with matchets through solid bamboo forest, a means
of progress unbelievably slow and tedious and so exhausting for the
matchet-wielders in front that reliefs for them became necessary
every quarter hour.

One evening No 29 found itself in harbour cheek by jowl with a
British column of 14 Brigade. Its officers proved to be despondent
men who made no bones about it. Gratifying as it might be that we
should have managed to keep intact all our column spirit and cohesion, relying on one another's strengths and to a lesser extent on a
shared capacity for manufacturing weak jokes out of the most
unpromising material, it remained little to boast of. Compared
with that of many battalions, our own battle experience had been
limited, our casualties in action light.

Rain, the irreconcilable foe, fell day and night, so much of it
indeed that the ground became thoroughly waterlogged and it took
the column hours to conquer hills which in May would have been
mounted at a canter. The stout-hearted Nigerians had repeatedly to
carry mule-loads on their heads to the hill tops. Two, possibly three
miles in a day became our outside limit, the sun wholly deserting
us, dry clothes a dream of wildest luxury, and worst of all the occasions when flames couldn't be conjured from soaking wood. To be
without hot tea or coffee meant deprivation indeed: what else had
we to look forward to? Supply drops became hopelessly irregular;
for three or four days in succession we subsisted on herbs gathered
by the indefatigable Kerens and boiled to make a thin and tasteless
soup. Any man who had saved biscuit or morsel of cheese from the
last ration drop would slink out of sight to eat it, unable to with-
stand the involuntary gaze of less provident comrades.

That during this starvation period I could think of nothing but
food was unremarkable: what surprised me was that my longings

should be concentrated not upon basic items such as K ration corned pork loaf, processed cheese or chocolate bar but on the finest, most profligate and elaborate meals ever consumed. Menus long forgotten returned to mind, flooding the memory; one could smell the food, see it steaming on the plate. I asked others if they too found themselves tortured by such visions. All did. We dreamed of rich meals in as sensual a way as contemporary gaolbirds might have dreamt of coupling with film stars.

The day's slog was enough and to spare for every men, but for certain members of the column (in addition to Corporal Sykes) it represented only a prelude to their real work – work having to be accomplished during the midday hour's halt, or in bivouac, at a time when every muscle and sinew, every brain-cell must have screamed for rest and sleep. Neil Leitch for one, assisted by his British medical sergeant and a few trained Africans, treated the sick by flashlight far into the darkness. How this quiet, rather withdrawn and highly intelligent man managed to do his job so humanely and with such devotion I cannot tell; he and his staff would be as tired as any before having a chance to look at patients. Neither the doctor nor his satellites possessed special privileges. They carried loads, footed it with the rest.

Captain Croasdell – 'Crow' – another creature of nocturnal or at least crepuscular habit, had as Animal Transport Officer and amateur vet the duty of making certain that mules and ponies were always properly cared for. Crow, round-faced and stocky, smiling and obstinate, performed it well. Galls and other ailments called for treatment; loads for each animal had to be checked constantly to ensure proper balance and adjustment. The mules were vital to us, radio sets our lifeline. Whenever an animal became a casualty mortar or machine gun ammunition, or heavy equipment, would perforce be jettisoned, one mule, in practical terms, more valuable than half a dozen soldiers, callous as so bald a statement may appear. Remarkably tough animals, mules supplemented their ration forage, dropped with ours, by eating bamboo shoots and other vegetation; few died of exhaustion but a number were to be killed by the enemy and by the end the surviving animals had become ghosts. The unfortunate ponies, refusing to look at anything but their forage and by comparison feeble beasts, collapsed and died one by one.

Arnold Mainprize, my staff officer, a gentle-natured Territorial, organised supply drop procedure and took a great deal off my shoulders, drafting returns and other signals and helping to look after general routine and detail, David Lewis, the administrative officer, assisted by a British colour sergeant, collected and collated requests for supply drop items. He had then to encode them – a lengthy business – for Corporal Sykes to send off to Air Base. All this, of course, while others rested. (Lewis, by profession a lawyer, seemed congenitally incapable of responding to the simplest of questions without a judicial pause of at least five seconds. Should his questioner be in a hurry, the delay might prove exasperating.)

Since Peter Vaughan, the bone of his upper arm shattered, remained ill and in great pain for some days after being wounded, Prichard, his staff officer, took over No 35 Column, Ricketts at his elbow should advice be needed. It wasn't long, however, before the ebullient Peter, officially hors de combat or not, began to take a more than cursory interest in his column's affairs. Poor Prichard, his decisions queried, his orders countermanded, hardly knew from hour to hour who was meant to be in charge and eventually Peter took over again de facto, which solved the problem at a stroke. While the situation had provided plenty of free entertainment for the rest of us, the hapless Prichard's brief experience of column command cannot have encouraged serious military ambitions.

During this march we heard over the radio that Brigadier Calvert had captured Mogaung with what remained of his columns after a fortnight of grim and costly attacks in appalling conditions, a feat of arms remarkable by any standards. Calvert's brigade, fighting almost continually since its arrival in Burma by glider, had been reduced to about half its original fighting strength before the battle for Mogaung had even reached the planning stage.

On one of the last days of this debilitating trek (which didn't in fact occupy us for quite so long as I imagine) we scrambled, famished, up to a Kachin village standing high on a hilltop. Grass as neat and richly green as an English lawn surrounded it and three majestic trees spread branches over the latticed huts under which hirsute pigs and piglets fled grunting and squealing for shelter when they saw us trudging in. All day we had as usual been drenched; but now the sun gleamed fitfully from a rain-washed sky and early the next morning we were rescued by the long-awaited supply drop. The lumbering Dakotas were the ravens that fed Elijah in the wilderness.

# CHAPTER 15

# Shots and Shells

As column commander I found myself a step or two removed from the Nigerian rank-and-file; my day-to-day orders went to officers. Such was the chain of command, close touch by word of mouth with individual soldiers less frequent now than when I had commanded companies in Nigeria and India. Much as I regretted this, what counted in Burma was not that our men happened to be black Africans, and therefore of special interest, but that they were comrades-in-arms. Colour and other racial differences signified little. We lived together, ate the same food, carried the same back-bending loads, suffered privation equally and fought literally side by side. The Nigerian in the ranks trusted his white officer or sergeant unreservedly and without question, neither complaining of his lot nor abandoning hope, but instead keeping alive a confidence and faith at times all but extinguished in the hearts of those he looked to. Sustaining hardship with equanimity, the worse the conditions the more fortitude the men displayed. As in their adaptation to the Burma forests, so in philosophic outlook our soldiers set us an example. It was a kindly provision of nature that allowed them so cleanly to wipe out memories of suffering or danger.

Thousands of miles separated the men we led from their homes in the West African savannah, from their women, their palm beer and feast-days, their black feudal lords. The Nigerians, willy nilly, found themselves in a forbidding country pitted against strangers altogether irrelevant to them, a people they hadn't known to exist and with whom they could have had no conceivable quarrel until we made our enmity theirs. The Japanese, ambitious and martial, were more than willing to die for an emperor they believed a god. The Nigerian soldiers, most of them peace-loving and none with the least urge for self-sacrifice, fought simply because they had promised their white leaders that they would. We imposed greatly upon their generosity.

On 2nd July, several days before either of the other two battalions, we reached the brigade rendezvous to find it clear of enemy. The goal towards which all had striven so arduously was hardly memorable. Pahok turned out to be nothing but four deserted huts in the jungle about fourteen miles west of Mogaung (in Chinese hands since Calvert had captured it).

No 35 Column became involved with a body of Japanese blocking the main track from Pahok to the railway valley, a track Ricketts had hoped to use as an evacuation route for sick and wounded. The casualties, no longer dragging behind us, had been left in a 'secure' haven some miles to the west where they could better be looked after until an escape route could be found. Peter's X Company, under its third commander, succeeded in dislodging the Japanese but satisfaction was much muted. Several Africans were killed and also No 35 Column's animal transport officer, Pip Haines, who had volunteered to fight because so many British junior leaders had become hors de combat. Refusing to take cover from point-blank enemy fire, Pip had paid in full. The Japanese had retreated, but how far wasn't known. It was not a safe route for stretchers.

In pursuit of an alternative the brigadier sent my column to drive off enemy reported to be occupying Hkamutyang, a Kachin village shown on the map as four or five miles to the south east, where either cross-tracks or a T junction was marked – one couldn't read which – one of these trails offering another path to the open valley for the sick and ultimately, perhaps, for ourselves. The mud on the track we followed, slippery and glutinous, was composed of pinkish-red earth reminiscent of the sandstone of South Devon cliffs and ploughland. Sliding round many a sticky twist and turn, I began to feel ridiculously nervous and expected ambush at every corner.

Three miles took us to a tiny hamlet called Nkum Pahok where I halted the column before having a careful look round. Though it was deserted by the living, MacFarlane and I felt shocked to discover huddled in a hut the blood-encrusted corpses of two aged Kachins, a man and a woman, murdered, we supposed, by Japanese soldiers for reasons of their own. Unloading the mules and shedding packs, we rested for a few minutes. A single scarlet hibiscus flower glowed amongst unkempt bushes and on impulse I stuck it in my hatband. But as symbol or gallant device the decoration went to waste: no sooner had we saddled up again than a message by runner from Brigade Headquarters postponed advance. Having succeeded by then in winding myself up in preparation for a fight, the order came to me as anticlimax rather than reprieve.

Many exhausting days of physical endeavour had passed since the column had exchanged so much as one shot with the enemy, and the wider the gap in time between actions the harder one found it to bridge.

We waited for two nights in Nkum Pahok, an interval without significance except for the ever willing Umoru Numan, behind a Bren gun, failing to kill or capture a solitary Japanese soldier approaching the huts. The Bren had jammed, but why on earth no other soldier had been able to stop the man I couldn't imagine.

Single Japanese were not uncommonly met with, but men of Chindit columns usually moved abroad in pairs when, for example, carrying messages along the dark and potentially hostile trails. Two men gave one another support, four eyes were better able to recognize a trap than two, and if one man should be killed or wounded the other might escape to tell the tale. But the Japanese soldier scorned companionship. He would patrol on his own; snipe determinedly for days, strapped to a tree; creep up alone to his enemy's position to observe or deliberately to draw fire; fight by himself to the death.

When word came to continue our move against Hkamutyang I made dispositions elaborately cautious. The escaped Japanese straggler must be assumed to have spread news of our presence and as Ram led his advanced guard along one of those alarming razor-edged ridge tracks we all too often had to follow, my imagination, running wild, pictured regiments of enemy waiting to pounce.

There wasn't one man. Reports of Jap troops had been false or out of date.

I found Ram waiting for me at a small T junction, frowning at his map, but while we agreed that this must be the place where 'Hkamutyang' was printed on it, neither Kachin nor hut was anywhere visible. The village had been spirited away. It was near dark; rapidly I posted platoons to cover all tracks, fresh boot-prints proclaiming that a body of Japanese had recently passed through. We settled for the night. Sykes erected the wireless aerial and I reported back to Brigade Headquarters; Arnold Mainprize produced his notebook and pencil; Idi Melor fussed about clearing the undergrowth round my hammock site and collecting firewood. Keyed up, apprehensive still, I took off pack and equipment and lit a cigarette.

A burst of Bren gun fire – two bursts – came from the left hand track fifty yards away. I froze, waiting. Silence. Striding up the track to discover what could have happened, I made out in the twilight half-averted African faces, sheepish as children's when caught doing something forbidden.

'What was this shooting? Where are the Japanese?' I almost shouted.

'It was one, sir – he walked up the path.'

'Where's the body?'

'He ran, sir. There is no body. He ran off at great speed. We didn't hit him. Truly this gun is not a good one.'

It was the day's second anti-climax and too much like the other stupid incident at Nkum Pahok. I had had enough. The sound of shooting so close had rattled me thoroughly and agitation gave place to humiliating rage. I could barely prevent myself from striking the Bren gunner and his friends for their incompetence.

No 35 Column with Peter Vaughan joined us on the 7th, which thickened the defences, while Brigade Headquarters, with the 6th and 12th Battalions, marched through our position and took the fork that led to the open valley. I stood by the track watching them tramp past, an endless procession of tired and overburdened men and mules covered with mud, led by officers several of whom I had known pretty well. Now they looked complete strangers: we had seen nothing of the other four Nigerian columns. After swapping shots with our Chinese allies – a result of Chinese error – and undertaking some fierce platoon actions against parties of enemy trying to block their way, the two battalions, reaching the valley south of Mogaung, met with resolute resistance from a hill by the roadside christened, I think by Ricketts, 'Hill 60' (of First War notoriety), its capture, so we understood, to signal the end of the campaign for the Nigerian Brigade unless Stilwell should have second thoughts, a possibility always on the cards.

On the day before the projected attack on Hill 60 by the 12th Battalion Sykes called me to the wireless to speak to the brigadier, whose urbane voice, distorted by atmospheric crackle, instructed me to take my fighting elements down into the valley early the following morning to block the road behind the hill and cut off the escape of any retreating Japanese.

'Rather you than me!' said a No 35 Column officer to Dicky Lambert.

'You windy man! When we're up to our flaming knees in mud and Jap bodies you'll wish you'd been there with us – or almost!' retorted Dicky.

'How does Brig Ricketts know there aren't as many Japs south of the hill as on top of it? Or more?'

The possibility had occurred to me as well; we lacked reliable information of any kind. Defeated by Calvert, followed up in their own good time by dawdling Chinese soldiers, such Japanese as remained in the Mogaung area would be dispersed in company and platoon groups, possibly out of touch with one another but undoubtedly capable of independent resistance to the end. I decided that the mortar must remain behind and that the machine gun detachments should leave their mules at Hkamutyang and manhandle weapons and ammunition, mules in the open making targets too conspicuous; but couldn't avoid taking one to carry the radio set which would keep me in touch with Brigade Headquarters.

The path we followed led directly to the east and within a bare half mile we were out of the forest. It was an hour after dawn; dazzled by the bright light all around us we blinked like owls in daytime, feeling as naked as woodland animals forced from their habitat. Weeks had gone by since we had last ventured into the open. Now we could see the whole vaulted sky, the flying birds, the moving clouds. Far to the north-east the mountains of Chinese Yunnan were indigo crayon smudges faint on the horizon.

It seemed long odds that we should be spotted before reaching the road or anywhere near it, our untidy procession, uniforms streaked with rust-coloured mud, as conspicuous as migrating wildebeeste against the knee-high grass. Which of various low hills we could see was the Hill 60 we must avoid? We had in fact been making straight for it, and in column snake at that, until providentially an African's sharp scouting eye detected signs of life on a mound, one bigger than most, four or five hundred yards directly ahead. Hastily I changed directions towards the south. Tramping across an enemy's front in full view constituted a manoeuvre that would have drawn withering criticism from the director of any peace-time exercise, but there was no help for it now. A quarter of a mile, possibly less, separated the head of the column from the banks of the Sahmaw stream, or chaung, where with luck we ought to be safer from observation. Though I continually glanced over my left shoulder at the hill, its few trees and crowning grass seemed innocent enough in spite of the soldier's report, and the leading rifle platoon had nearly gained the stream before I turned for a last look. It was dotted all over with little brown objects.

'Arnold,' I said, pointing. 'Take a look at those things. They must be men.'

'Those? I don't think so – no. Aren't they bushes?'

Glancing at me doubtfully, Mainprize stroked his beard. I

looked away and then, like a child playing grandmother's steps, quickly turned my head. Several of the brown things moved. Without a shadow of doubt they were soldiers, standing about in groups now and watching us with interest.

'You were right,' said Arnold Mainprize, convinced. 'Must be part of some column or other. Can't be Japs or we'd have known all about it by now!'

Might not these figures, uniforms reddish-brown with mud, like ours, indeed be friendly troops, perhaps Chinese?

My leading riflemen were beginning to clamber down the stream bank when machine guns opened fire. Their bursts short and tentative at first, the gunners on the hill appeared uncertain. But soon enough the regular, slow beat began to hammer the air, a succession of bullets cracking overhead like whips and trimming the grass at our feet. One or two men fell. I shouted that everybody must keep moving, on no account go to ground, and after an age all had reached the banks of the Sahmaw chaung. We found them less deep than I had hoped they would be. Popping in and out of view like snap-targets on a rifle range as under partial cover it made its way in single file towards the road, each platoon in turn provided splendid practice for the enemy machine guns. Missiles from grenade-dischargers, exploding prettily in puffs of delicate blue smoke, fell some yards short but added to the din.

Then, suddenly and astonishingly, as at a word of command all shooting stopped. Possibly the enemy now found himself as dubious of our identity as we had been of his, though to a Japanese officer peering through field glasses our bush hats must have labelled us unambiguously. But red figures still crowded the hill; under cover of overhead machine gun fire they might, I believed, be contemplating some reckless advance against our strung-out procession and I gave orders to halt, positioning the rifle platoons so as to face Hill 60, the stream a little way behind them and the Vickers guns to one flank. Every move must have been observed by the watchers, but they took no action. Not another shot was fired. Puzzled, confused, for the first time in the campaign I pulled out my binoculars. The damp and dirt fogging the lenses reflected the cumulative fatigue that fogged my mind and now robbed me of my wits. Could the blurred, muddy shapes I saw really be Japanese? Was it quite certain? Regardless or forgetful of the weapons used against us, I hesitated to order our own guns to open up until I had satisfied myself beyond all doubt.

At this stage the officer in charge of the two Vickers ran up to the bush by which I stood peering through my useless field glasses. He was very excited, face vivid with anticipation. Seldom had Hay-Coghlan been given the chance to fire his guns.

'Let me loose off a belt of two, sir! What a lovely target – they're asking for it! They're bloody Japs all right.'

Of course they were. Coggie's statement resolved my ludicrous dilemma once and for all.

'Shoot as soon as you can,' I told him.

Steady bursts from our two Vickers machine guns, heartening as the music of a regimental band, encouraged us all. Ram, John and I, together with our orderlies and all foolishly in one bunch, stood absorbed, watching Japanese troops bolting like rabbits into the burrows of their human warren. We must have made a tempting target. An answering burst of fire aimed in our direction, whipping past so perilously close that one could almost smell the bullets, compelled – of course too late – a simultaneous dive to earth. As soon as we got to our feet a second burst greeted us and Ram's orderly fell. The blood trickling down his smooth black thigh looked curiously unreal and out of place, as though it were red paint. We carried Ali below the stream bank where a number of other Africans hurt earlier lay mute, some stoically smoking the cigarettes inseparable from lightly wounded soldiers of any nationality.

First checks indicated that no more than four men had been killed, their bodies lying somewhere in the open concealed by long grass. It was extraordinary that we should have suffered casualties so light. The enemy, initially at any rate, had been presented with a target which, in the professional idiom, was a machine gunner's dream and had failed to take advantage of it.

We found ourselves not far from where we were supposed to be and I sent Sergeant Umoru Numan with a few men to creep along under the bank and have a look at the road. It ran, he reported back, about two or three hundred yards to our right and was certainly enemy-held, as was the line of the Sahmaw stream on the other side of it. Thus both we and the Japanese held sections of its bank and faced in exactly the same direction, surely an odd circumstance. The machine guns having missed Sykes' mule, I reported our location to a vague Brigade Headquarters, eventually to be told that the attack on Hill 60 had failed but that a second was scheduled for the following day, this time after a Chinese artillery bombardment. Meanwhile we were to remain in situ, a prospect which failed to please. As at

Ponhon months before, we had expected to return to our base before dark and left there packs and blankets, groundsheets and most of our rations.

The marshy ground occupied by the riflemen turned out to be so sodden that attempted shelter-holes immediately became pools of water; platoons were compelled to lie out in the open unprotected. Towards sunset the Japanese on Hill 60 took it into their heads to fire haphazardly in our direction and a wounded man was carried into my headquarters under the bank, a location shared with the 'Aid Post' and on the following day by the mortar detachment also. The bullet had penetrated just below this man's eye to emerge at the back of his head, and after a single glance Bowen, Neil Leitch's white medical sergeant, shrugged his shoulders. Yet a quarter of an hour later the soldier was puffing a cigarette. That life should have been restored to him when to all appearances he was dying – should indeed have died by now – seemed miracle rather than physiological fluke.

Next morning, after a more or less sleepless night, we watched shell-bursts from a Chinese-manned American howitzer blanket like fog the green hill in front of us preliminary to the Nigerian attack from the other side. Few men, I thought ingenuously, could survive such heavy and concentrated fire, but without aircraft it wasn't enough; and when the pounding ceased we heard the drumbeat of enemy machine guns firing north. After dropping a succession of mortar bombs on Hill 60, we waited, ready to undertake whatever else might be required of us when the moment seemed ripe, but neither shouts nor African cheering reached our ears and after a while the Japanese guns stopped firing. Evidently the attack had failed.

Though tormenting mosquitoes and midges again made sleep next to impossible the second night passed quietly enough and early in the morning, just as we were about to pack up, I was surprised by a visitor, the Colonel himself. Peter seemed near to fainting with exhaustion, his wound unhealed and painful, the bone of the upper arm now dangerously infected. The trek from Hkamutyang, very risky and undertaken without a guide, must have tried him severely and for several minutes he could scarcely speak. Yet Peter, in typically gallant and generous style, had left his own column to see for himself what he could do to help, having already, the previous day, sent us men carrying food, a mortar and a supply of bombs. Were our situations reversed, I the sick and wounded colonel and Peter the commander of the junior column, would I have been capable of summoning the will and guts to do as much for him? Guiltily I remembered that when occasionally I felt opposed to my Commanding Officer's decisions I hadn't failed to let him know it. Peter put me to shame.

Without further adventure we returned to Hkamutyang via the Sahmaw chaung, a route which gave Hill 60 a wider berth, and began to feel more at ease immediately the forest had swallowed us. We heard that the second attempt by the 12th Battalion on Hill 60 had succeeded initially, the top momentarily gained but the Nigerians thrown off it by a counter-attack from the south-east side. Abdy Ricketts, who saw as little merit as Calvert in commanding from the rear, had been in the thick of things and received a slight grenade wound to show for it. The failures at Hill 60 proved time-consuming: the Japanese obstinately refused to be 'winkled out with the bayonet,' a fate the Brigadier had confidently predicted for them, and for days afterwards the knoll held out; it was, eventually, found to be as honey-combed with subterranean passages as a gigantic badger's sett. Battered constantly by aircraft, by American-Chinese howitzers and Nigerian and Chinese mortars, a comparatively small number of Japanese defenders, presumed on the point of starvation, stuck to their suicidal task with a courage and tenacity beyond emulation.

An evacuation channel for sick and wounded who reached the valley had meanwhile been opened. North of Hill 60 American light-planes, and even motor ambulances, were at hand on the Kamaing road. All columns had been assured daily for weeks that Myitkyina, an important town on the railway eighty miles north of Mogaung, was just about to fall to our allies, the continual announcements becoming a sour Chindit joke; but now that the Japanese garrison had finally been compelled by Stilwell's Chinese and Americans to evacuate the place the news became of significance. Myitkyina possessed an all-weather airstrip from which we could be flown out.

Peter Vaughan, my superior and friend, warned by Dr Bob Murray that he would lose his arm if he resisted further, finally exchanged his battalion for a hospital bed in India, Arnold Mainprize moving over to look after No 35 until Nobby Hall, recovered from his wound, got himself flown in again to head the column he had so well served. The brigadier, however, wouldn't return the gentle Arnold to me and I missed his conciliatory demeanour and misleadingly fierce beard. (A month later Arnold allowed me to see the brief campaign diary he had kept. I noticed that two entries read: 'Charles being difficult today.')

Soon after our own empty-handed return from the Sahmaw riverbank No 35 Column trudged off to join the other two battalions north of Hill 60, where it remained in reserve. The brigadier ordered mine to stay put at Hkamutyang.

For two or three days the sun shone brilliantly from azure skies, butterflies, very large and handsome ones, sailing across forest clearings and settling on the ground like bright fallen flowers to imbibe moisture from the fresher mule droppings. Although I should have liked to capture a few for later identification I restrained myself. The Nigerians – perhaps some of the remaining British – might have interpreted such antics as plain evidence that their commander was cracking under the strain; but when rain returned to drench us and the butterflies disappeared I was to regret my lack of moral courage.

None of us could pretend to be spoiling for a fight. There seemed a fair chance now that those officers and men who had managed to keep going without becoming casualties of one kind or another would return to India. Privation, physical exhaustion and the erosion of nervous stress, combined with an eye to deliverance, had between them extinguished that spark that makes fresh, well-trained soldiers eager for battle to prove ability and manhood. We had become lethargic, content to carry out the letter of orders without looking for windmills to tilt at. These orders were to sit tight in order to protect the brigade flank, and more importantly to hold open the path to safety for the few wounded and many sick who still lay to our west in the Kachin hills.

Peace was broken before long. At two o'clock one morning shooting from the direction of the forward rifle platoons wakened the rest of the column and everybody 'stood to'. Under Ram and Dicky a couple of platoons, dug in amongst lantana on the very edge of the forest, sat astride the path we followed when, venturing into the open, we had nearly walked into Hill 60. They lay about half a mile from Column Headquarters, runner the one means of communication. I had no idea what might be happening, our walky-talky radios having long since packed up; but after a while shooting ceased. Before dawn it broke out again, and more vociferously. The African orderlies at Column Headquarters, deep sleepers all, stirred, coughed and muttered until, prodded awake by the African sergeant-major, once more they stood to arms until the noise of battle died.

As soon as there was light enough to see by I walked gingerly down the track, feeling naked and exposed but meeting nothing until I caught sight of Ram and Dicky at the foot of the hill. They looked like buccaneers, brims of bush hats bent and twisted, uniforms and faces filthy, primed grenades hung dangerously on belts and carbines in hand. Their faces reassured me at once. My heart stopped pounding.

A platoon or more of Japanese had clashed with Ram's Africans, though whether our enemy had originally intended a deliberate attack remained uncertain. Possibly not; they might have been sent to hold the very track junction we lay astride and blundered into Ram's troops by accident. Before dawn, however, the Japanese had seriously attempted to force a passage, approaching to within five yards, but after a deal of firing and noisy demonstration abandoned the effort. The enemy, in worse straits than we, must have been exhausted, disease-ridden, hungrier and with no hope of succour. As a rule the Japanese showed themselves resolute and mobile at night and considerably more enterprising than Allied troops, darkness a shield against our aircraft. Nigerians, on the other hand, were prone to become clumsy and anxious: night a time ordained by Allah for making love in a warm hut, dancing round a bonfire, singing or sleeping; evil spirits likely to be abroad in bush and jungle.

The possibility of some unsteadiness in face of enemy night activity had always been a worry at the back of my mind and it came as a great relief that under Ram's level-headed leadership the two rifle platoons should creditably have held off the Japanese. They – the enemy – hadn't retired altogether and seemed to be engaged in digging a position for themselves on a low hill in the open about a furlong from where we three were standing. To know that Japanese remained within shouting distance was bound to impose an extra strain on the nerves of the tired men in the two forward platoons, but the ground the enemy apparently intended holding would be useless from their point of view, rendering them incapable either of impeding the passage of the sick to safety or of interfering with the column should it be ordered to join the rest of the brigade. The Japanese sat astride the wrong track. Though neither then nor subsequently had I the least intention of attacking them across open ground with the certainty of incurring casualties for no good tactical reason, we could at least mortar the digging Japanese and I promised Ram that it would be done.

In a glade near Column Headquarters the stout mortar stood in its shallow pit. John Murray, my very young and quiet mortar officer, anticipating events, had made his calculations some days before and aligned his weapon ready to shoot in front of Ram's platoons. Standing directly behind the elevated barrel, I watched the first bombs rush high into the sky until at the top of their flight they had become small flung pebbles in the distance before changing direction to plunge like meteorites to earth. At first it was a slow business; Murray had to rely on written notes from Ram for correcting his aim. Tell-tale white wisps from the muzzle, visible from a distance to a watchful eye, drifted over the tree tops and in ten minutes we heard the faint pop of a hostile mortar from the vicinity of the Sahmaw chaung. There followed a general scuttle, every African in sight by his foxhole, waiting to hear how close the first bomb might be going to fall. Whistling mournfully out of the sky, it exploded in the bamboos a little way down the slope south of Column Headquarters, those succeeding, crashing down every minute, landing too close to be ignored but not close enough to harm us.

Both mortars, ours and theirs, as though by telepathic agreement ceased firing within a few moments of each other. The sun appeared; cicadas tuned up for a brief midday concert and at Column Headquarters we sat basking and smoking, opening K ration tins and undoing cellophane biscuit wrappings. To prevent our position being registered more accurately I placed a veto on fires throughout the column.

After a quick breakfast, reckoning that the enemy troops would be on their feet digging vigorously we opened up again with the mortar, but when a long file of escorted stretcher-bearers walked through the rear of our position on their way to the light-planes and ambulances, I ordered John Murray to stop shooting. Should the enemy decide to retaliate before the sick had got clear it needed no imagination to picture the stretcher-bearers dropping their human burdens and bolting for cover. The minutes crawled, the convoy of sick endless, its pace that of a tortoise. Efforts to hasten the bearers failed; they were already doing their best and had I betrayed too emphatic an impatience would perhaps have shown greater concern for their own skins than their patients'.

The last stretcher hadn't got two hundred yards beyond our position before the Japanese showed their hand, their weapon this time a small high-velocity field gun which spat like a cat. The first shell arrived with the gun's report and before we had time to jump into

our slit trenches, a couple of dozen following it at very brief intervals. From my pit I caught a glimpse of fluttering green pennants on
bamboo lances drooping and falling as metal fragments severed the
canes and felt again the vivid apprehension and fear, the suspended
instants of time between shot and shell I remembered at White
City. But, unlike the coal-scuttle dramas, this turned out no prolonged affair. The bombardment was violent but brief. When it
ceased we waited for a minute, then clumsily emerged from our pits
like paleolithic men from caves, unkempt, dirty, covered in red
mud and no doubt rank-smelling as our ancestors. None of us had
bathed for weeks.

Though capable of life-saving inaccuracy when they peered at us
through the sights of machine gun or rifle, the Japanese handled
artillery and mortars with great skill. How they had come to pinpoint so cleverly where Column Headquarters was I couldn't
understand, unless it were a lucky fluke or some unseen watcher
had spied on us. Nearly every shell had fallen slap into the space,
not more than fifty yards in diameter, occupied by my headquarters officers and men, the acrid fumes of cordite, infesting the
bushes, almost tangible. Three of Corporal Sykes' wireless mules
lay dead. Stretched stiffly on the mud near the main path, they
looked like stuffed beasts ready for setting up in glass cases.

'They've killed them, sir,' I think I remember Sykes saying. He
was heartbroken.

The day continued eventful. Towards sunset a Japanese scout,
foolishly walking into Ramsay's position, was shot dead, his possessions sent to Column Headquarters as a matter of routine for John
MacFarlane (as intelligence officer) and I to have a look at. Without
much interest we began to examine the cotton body-belt of sewn-in
charms, the paybook, identity discs and bright picture postcards of
cherry blossom and Mount Fujiyama, all more or less standard
items. Then my eye was caught by a leather wallet, carefully
wrapped up to protect it from wet. It contained photographs, not
snapshots but professionally taken pictures. There was one of a
round-faced girl, smiling, white flowers tucked in her hair; another
of a wrinkled couple sitting stiffly, formally upright on a bench; a
third of a young officer in what looked to be brand-new uniform,
curved sword at hip.

I gazed at each picture in turn until the light faded and it was time
for 'stand to'. From the moment of stepping out of our Dakota on
the White City airstrip I had regarded Japanese as nothing but

dangerous vermin whom it was our job to destroy if we could; Japanese courage – unquenchable, unyielding – the courage of some predatory animal rather than a man's, Japanese cruelty and ruthlessness not propaganda distortion but attended truth. Now, faced with this pathetic evidence of our common humanity, forced to acknowledge that the gulf between us could not after all be fundamental, I felt as much cheated as moved.

# CHAPTER 16

# Farewell to the Green Hills

Enemy shells and bombs, replied to by the one mortar we had, burst about our positions at some period of every day, making us unwilling to stray too far from foxholes. Among the few killed and wounded was Sergeant Bowen, Neil's assistant, he who at the Sahmaw chaung had despaired of the African shot through the head. A shell exploded in the Aid Post, which only the previous day had been filled with wounded and sick. The column was well dug-in and casualties light; but at this stage the loss of a single soldier, particularly a man struck down from a distance while crouching passively, unheroically in a hole in the ground with no opportunity to retaliate, seemed damnable. The mule ranks became gradually thinned out, the poor animals, though kept tethered in hollows, standing upright and sadly vulnerable wherever they might be placed. Their carcases, bloated, buzzing with flies, smelling abominably but too heavy to shift or bury, poisoned the air. Earlier in the campaign the death of such a number would have spelt disaster. Twice the Japanese from their mound opposite Ram's and Dicky's men let off ragged rifle volleys for much of the night, presumably to get rid of surplus ammunition, but did no physical harm and went unanswered. Flies, a further reminder of White City days and blithely impervious to rain, alighted in black squadrons on food and faces. My ban on fires remained. Since downpours were many and tinder sodden, the clouds of smoke issuing from wet fuel would, I decided, too boldly advertise our whereabouts. In the face of mounting evidence that the enemy gunners and mortarmen knew precisely where we were located it was a faint-hearted decision, little gained by so dismal a sacrifice and much lost: hot drinks, hot meals and fires to dry clothes couldn't fail to have lightened spirits. Two months, even one month earlier I might have shown less timidity.

At one point during this depressing period I needed a British officer or sergeant to take out a small and not particularly dangerous reconnaissance patrol. White leaders commanding fighting groups were by now so woefully reduced in number, and had already done so much, that I decided to give the task to a young specialist sergeant of my Headquarters staff. Through no fault of his, he had had very little to do and been involved in no fight or skirmish.

Having sent for Sergeant Bartley (not his true name), I told him what I wanted done and how to go about it. Bartley remained silent. I observed that beads of sweat shone on his forehead and in his eyes stood fear. His hands were shaking, his face white.

'I can't do it sir,' he mumbled at last.

'Can't do it? What on earth do you mean?' I was astonished.

'I couldn't face it, sir.'

'But it's nothing, man! Of course you can face it – don't talk such nonsense.'

'I can't, sir. Honestly. It's no use . . .'

I could get little more out of the poor man – indeed scarcely needed to. Voice, appearance, nervous tremors told all. To rage, to try to bully or threaten him into carrying out the task seemed to me futile: Bartley's uncontrolled fear would certainly have infected the Africans with him, nothing be gained and much lost. He might – probably would – have concealed himself and his men fifty yards from our positions, waited awhile and then returned with some cock-and-bull story. The tale of a British 'Sergy' having become incapacitated through fear would have spread throughout the column.

'Are you ill, Sergeant Bartley?' I asked finally.

'No, sir – I don't think so, sir.'

'You will report to Captain Leitch with a note I'll give you in a minute, and if he says you're fit for duty I shall send you to the brigade commander at Hill 60. You'll have to get there on your own.'

Neil Leitch found nothing physically the matter with Bartley. That same day he went off by himself to Brigade Headquarters, carrying my written message detailing the circumstances and recommending that the sergeant be flown out. There existed a precedent for this: Peter Vaughan had sent back to India from White City, in May, a failed white man from No 35 Column. Brigadier Ricketts, however, decided that Bartley couldn't be allowed to 'get away with it altogether' while his comrades were still facing the enemy and employed him at the brigade supply dropping zone, where he could make himself useful without having to expose his pitiably broken nerve for all to see. It was a humane solution.

I must confess to having felt scant sympathy for Bartley: his breakdown shocked me. Never before required to do anything positive, he had lost his nerve utterly as soon as some action had been asked of him. I didn't stop to consider – nor ought to have allowed it to influence me if I had – whether months of very nervous passivity might not have undermined such native will-power as Bartley possessed.

We find it hard to forgive or excuse in others the manifestation of a weakness we know to exist in ourselves; but I doubt if this came into it. My concern was a great deal less for Bartley than for my column, for the whole tree rather than a single bough.

Brought low for the second time by a mild bout of fever, I grew listless and depressed, doubts flocking round me like crows. The presence of Hay-Coughlan the machine gunner, now column staff officer in place of Arnold Mainprize (who had returned to No 35 Column), and John MacFarlane was comforting. Coggie, invariably cheerful, a worldly man well into his thirties, managed to combine cynicism with a sanguine temperament; John, quieter but by no means dour, full of good sense and humour. He and I happened to have been contemporaries at the same preparatory school and in my mind's eye there remained a picture of John running down a soccer pitch trying ineffectually to control the ball; a small, thin boy of ten all arms and legs and with a plate.

The brigadier, who hadn't forgotten No 29 Column in his pre-occupation with Hill 60, suggested in the course of a wireless conversation that fighter-bombers ought to rid us of the Japanese troops still sitting in front of our position. Having endured ten days of ceaseless strain, Ram's two platoons had been relieved by soldiers from the 6th. So obvious and straightforward a solution hadn't occurred to me. Instead of welcoming the idea, I at first stubbornly refused to consider it, in my head some hazy notion that, sink or swim, we must manage things for ourselves unaided by brigadiers or aircraft. But the tactful Ricketts patiently insisted. He must have thought I had lost my senses.

The Mustang fighters appeared overhead on the next fine morning and we of Column HQ moved half a mile down the slope to obtain a good view. John Murray dropped mortar smoke bombs to indicate the target and we made radio contact with the American flight leader. I listened through earphones to a confident drawl exactly like the voice of some cinema hero whose name, eluding me, exercised my memory for days afterwards. For a minute or two the aircraft circled the smoke, like birds of prey over a bush fire, then one by one they dived, almost brushing the trees above us before letting fall twin bombs from their wings. There followed tremendous concussions, blast waves almost knocking us off our feet and red earth bespattering the sky above the Japanese position. Again the Mustangs dived, machine-gunning; orange flames, the breath of dragons, spurted from wing roots and metal clips and hot cartridge cases showered down. It was over in a few minutes. The leader wished us luck.

'Call us again if you're in trouble, boys,' he said.

Later on some of us had a look at the cratered position, which bore every mark of having been hastily abandoned. Just recognisable as narrow humps we found graves not newly dug, demonstrating that Ram's platoons, John Murray's mortar or both must have taken toll. Black grenade-discharger bombs with brightly painted rings, rifle ammunition and other debris lay scattered about and I picked up a piece of paper on which had been drawn a plan of the defences. Meticulously penned in coloured inks, it depicted foxholes, the emplácements of light machine guns with their arcs of fire, reserve positions, every conceivable military detail. The artist, presumably the Japanese officer in command, couldn't have prepared his plan more neatly had he been sitting in Rangoon.

With the enemy infantry vanished also his supporting guns and mortars. Tormented by them no longer we lit fires again, relishing the long-denied luxury of hot drinks, dry clothes and, in the evenings, occasional tots of rum. (The brigade supply dropping organisation north of Hill 60 had kept us in rations: for six columns all within a mile or two of one another a single dropping zone enough.) Ram and Dicky took it in turns to join us at Column Headquarters and together we would sit drinking and talking and adding fresh verses to our scurrilous songs, oblivious to the soured surroundings and evil stench of dead mules. For a while the miseries of rain and mud and hunger would be forgotten; in our hearts we would feel the old sense of dedication, of high adventure with which we had first set out and never wholly lost.

Very soon after the Mustangs' visit I heard over the radio from Brigade Headquarters that Hill 60 had fallen to a battalion of the newly arrived British 36th Division, supported by Nigerians. A 'conventional' formation, this division had been directed to regain control of the railway corridor that many Chindits had fought and died in, dominated for a period and then abandoned on the orders of General Stilwell, who given a free hand would surely have insisted on those of us still upright staying on in Burma until none survived to tell his tale.

Ricketts, as I had anticipated, instructed me to bring No 29

Column to join the rest of the brigade on Hill 60. We stumbled away from sordid Hkamutyang, as usual sweating copiously after the respite from pack-carrying. The brigadier met me on the captured Japanese position and directed the column to dig foxholes at the foot of the slope in marshy, insalubrious-looking ground. I didn't like the place at all. The hilltop itself, earth churned up as by a giant bulldozer, had been pounded almost out of shape. Dead enemy, fly-spotted, resembling discarded waxwork figures, lay here and there, one body with a Japanese bayonet still attached to its rifle buried deep in its skull. Had the soldier, in agony, implored a comrade to finish him off? If so, it seemed a remarkably brutal way of going about it. Equally the man might have tried to run, surrender or been guilty of other human frailty that in Japanese eyes amounted to cowardice deserving summary execution. An academic point, it was one impossible to decide.

Close to Hill 60 a number of British troops from the new division, neat, clean and pink-cheeked and bearing no resemblance to Chindit soldiers, were on their feet waiting for orders. Their officers, armed with nothing more lethal than ashplants, looked as though about to take part in a military exercise at Aldershot. Some of us were standing a little way off, examining the newcomers with interest, when a lone Japanese machine gun chanced to open up from the Sahmaw direction. The whole party flung themselves to the ground as one man, and we gazed at them in wonder. When the gun ceased its bass beat the British troops scrambled sheepishly to their feet, clearly embarrassed to see that none of us had moved an inch. There had been no need; the bullets had cracked past forty yards from the nearest soldier. It was a petty triumph for experience.

Abdy Ricketts asked me to join him for a K ration breakfast the following morning. His manner clearly indicated that he had something to tell me; and so deep was the slough of despond into which I had suddenly plunged since leaving Hkamutyang that although he had never given a hint of such a belief, I became convinced the brigadier meant to say that he had found me wanting, and who in a better position to judge? Feeling like a condemned man awaiting his life sentence, I presented myself at the hour requested. After some well-mannered circumlocution Brigadier Ricketts brought himself to the point and numbly I awaited his pronouncement of doom.

'Charles,' he said gently, fondling his thick black beard, 'when I pointed out to you yesterday where I wanted your column, you said loudly and in front of your officers that it was a bloody awful spot I'd chosen! You didn't even wait until my back was turned. Now I know you're very tired – we all are – but that's hardly the sort of thing to say, is it?'

For several moments I stared at my brigadier in blank bewilderment, unable to take in what he had said. Then, pulling myself together, I apologised for yesterday's thoughtless rudeness (which I had entirely forgotten), so overwhelmed with relief that had I been standing up instead of sitting on the ground I think I might have fallen.

Later that morning Shaw, the taciturn and imaginative colour sergeant of my old 10th Battalion B Company, came to see me. I had no idea he was in Burma. Tall, emaciated and so heavily bewhiskered that I failed to recognise him, Shaw was forty-one, surely the oldest man in the Nigerian Brigade. Ever eager for new experiences, as a volunteer reinforcement he had willingly dropped rank to sergeant in order to become a Chindit, and as I was the devil he knew had tried his hardest to join No 29 Column. Instead he had been sent to the 12th at White City. Shaw's familiar voice vividly recalled Kaduna days. What, I wondered, had become of B Company?*

After sending out a party to find and decently bury the men killed by the Japanese machine guns days before by the Sahmaw chaung, with John (or was it Ram?) I walked a mile south down the uncomfortably open valley to visit a couple of Z Company platoons detailed to repair the road for vehicles of the British 36th Division (about to move south) and attempt a landing strip with stones collected out of a stream, Ram indignant that his weary soldiers should be employed on a task he judged impracticable. The Divisional Commander himself appeared out of the blue as we were watching the labouring Nigerians. We saluted, more or less smartly.

'Ha!' he said. 'What are you two up to? Rubbernecking – sightseeing – I suppose!'

On the face of it this might have been taken as a remark innocent enough, but the Divisional Commander's brusque-bluff, faintly

---

*    It was to fight in the Arakan, under Ricketts himself as brigadier. I heard many months later that my successor, Karlshoven, had been awarded the Military Cross and Yaro Zuru, my favourite sergeant, the Military Medal.

James Shaw subsequently wrote an excellent book about his experiences with the 12th, *The March Out* (Hart-Davis 1953).

patronising manner as he uttered it grated on us both. There he stood with his red hat on, the archetypal general, a commanding figure, four-square. Though not a week can have elapsed since his own arrival at what fighting soldiers call 'the sharp end', he seemed to be accusing us in so many words of entertaining ourselves with an idle afternoon's stroll instead of going about our business. Regrettably I lacked courage to make a suitably insubordinate retort.

'No, sir,' I replied, 'these are my men working here.'

'Humph,' he grunted as he strode off with his staff officer.

Protesting vigorously but in vain, the three Nigerian battalions were ordered to hand over surviving mules to one of the new British brigades, a decision which however sensible from a military point of view caused grief and resentment. Our enduring and stalwart animals deserved at least a month of rest and plenty; we had looked forward to bringing them back to India and spoiling them. The black muleteers were desolate, many weeping.

After the 7th August, on which night came heavy but inaccurate Japanese shelling, nothing much happened. The brigadier ordered machine gun and mortar practice shoots, perhaps to entertain the gun crews, and arranged for a group photograph to be taken of the remaining British of his battalions on top of Hill 60. I don't think I ever saw the print.

At this stage the powerful reaction following upon release from constant tension now depressed and enervated me to such an extent that my legs turned to putty. The prospect of imminent deliverance failed to raise my spirits by a single degree; the least physical or mental effort became an intolerable burden. On 15th August, the day before we were due to march the fourteen miles to Mogaung, en route for Myitkyina airfield, for good measure I developed a high fever, but decided that if I could possibly manage it I must take the column out to India myself rather than surrender to the doctors at the last moment. After remaining on my feet thus far, abdication would have been ignominious.

I felt in no physical or mental state to notice much during that last march. Insufferably hot though we found it tramping along an open, rutted road under the sun's brassy stare, I don't think many soldiers dropped out, even if aware that they would be picked up not by the enemy but by a friendly ambulance. Near Mogaung my eye was caught and held by a Japanese skull stuck on top of a post by the roadside, with a placard nailed below it on which was written 'I AINT GOT NO BODY'. Did this grisly memorial represent American humour?

Having just managed to reach Mogaung I felt incapable of further exertion and left every administrative arrangement to what remained of the column staff, sleeping whenever possible. Eventually we boarded railway carriages. Seats and standing room inside were reserved for us but the outside of every carriage swarmed with truculent Chinese soldiers clinging to door handles or anything else they could find and lying on the roofs in close-packed shoals. Had we been unarmed they would, I felt sure, have fought us for seats. The engine of the train, a jeep – or perhaps several – fitted with locomotive wheels, had by some magical means to pull grossly over-loaded carriages eighty miles to Myitkyina. Not long after we were under way bursts of delighted laughter came from the Chinese hitchers: one of their number had broken his arm against a tree or telephone pole. What was in their eyes a splendidly comical incident dispelled every vestige of their previous ill-humour.

At Myitkyina, that day or the next, the men of No 29 Column climbed into Dakotas and were flown to Assam, the beautiful, equivocal green forests of Upper Burma innocuous under our wings. Weakly I gave away Japanese rifle cartridges, grenade discharger bombs, the coloured diagram of the enemy position opposite ours at Hkamutyang – indeed every item I had methodically hoarded during the past week – to the American pilot, retaining just wit enough not to declare the silk flag salvaged from the ambush. These pilots, obsessive souvenir hunters to a man, preyed upon returning Chindits easily coaxed into parting with hard-won trophies to their saviours.

What I longed for most was a bed, and where in Assam our air-craft landed I cannot recall. It was a matter of complete indif-ference. But I do remember giving the order to march to attention in threes, rifles at the slope and slings tight, as we approached the tented camp prepared for the reception of returning columns. However filthy, tattered and worn-out, I felt it important that we should look like soldiers still and make as brave a show as possible.

# Postscript

A couple of months after flying out, the 7th Battalion (I was by then in command) found itself, in company with the Royal Leicesters and 3rd/6th Gurkhas, once again in an Indian jungle camp, busily retraining enthusiastically for future operations under a capable brigadier, Wilkinson of the Leicesters, who had fought a fine defensive battle against the Japanese by Indaw lake. We might have saved our energy; to our great grief the Chindit 'Special Force' was broken up. There was no Wingate to fight for its survival when General Slim came to the conclusion that no rôle remained for Chindits either in Burma or further east. Although at one stage, on impulse and without consulting anybody, I volunteered the battalion as parachutists, nothing came of it and finally our Nigerian soldiers returned to their homeland without further warlike excursion and I to England.

# Index